THE RIDDLE OF LIFE

The Riddle of Life

J. H. BAVINCK

Translated by Bert Hielema

WILLIAM B. EERDMANS PUBLISHING COMPANY
GRAND RAPIDS, MICHIGAN

Wm. B. Eerdmans Publishing Co.
2140 Oak Industrial Drive N.E., Grand Rapids, Michigan 49505
© 2016 Wm. B. Eerdmans Publishing Co.
All rights reserved
Published 2016

Library of Congress Cataloging-in-Publication Data

Names: Bavinck, J. H. (Johan Herman), 1895-1964, author.
Title: The riddle of life / J. H. Bavinck; translated by Bert Hielema.
Other titles: Raadsel van ons leven. English
Description: Grand Rapids, Michigan: Eerdmans Publishing Company, 2016.
Identifiers: LCCN 2016003795 | ISBN 9780802873330 (pbk.: alk. paper)
Subjects: LCSH: Life—Religious aspects—Christianity. |
Theological anthropology—Christianity.
Classification: LCC BV4509.5 .B392513 2016 | DDC 233—dc23
LC record available at http://lccn.loc.gov/2016003795

www.eerdmans.com

Contents

	Translator's Note	vii
1.	The Great Awakening	1
2.	What Do We Know?	6
3.	Faith	11
4.	The World Order	17
5.	Where Do We Come From?	22
6.	Who Are We?	27
7.	The Meaning of Life	31
8.	God's Plan: The Grand Chess Game	36
9.	Our Idols: Money	41
10.	Our Idols: Honor	47
11.	Our Idols: The Pursuit of Pleasure	53
12.	Sin	59
13.	The Cry for Deliverance	63
14.	The Redeemer	68

15. Jesus, the Redeemer	72
16. The Offered Salvation	80
17. Why We Are Here	84
18. The Completion of Life	90

Translator's Note

This book, which was written before 1940 – the first edition came out in 1940 – is a popular version of the later *Between the Beginning and the End*. It was published seventy-five years ago by the longtime publisher J. H. Kok N. V., Kampen, and there continues to be a lively interest in the book in the Netherlands.

The book is entirely written in a casual way – no theological jargon – an aspect I have preserved in my translation, making it an easy and pleasing read. Bavinck was primarily a missionary, a man trying to reach the unconverted, but his message still has much to offer to readers today.

Bert Hielema

CHAPTER ONE

The Great Awakening

When we for the first time are consciously aware of what really is going on in the world, and therefore suddenly look at the world with renewed eyes, that is the precise moment when we are overwhelmed with questions. Why? Because the problems that confront us today are so numerous and in the main so intractable that, while trying to solve them, we cannot escape the distinct notion that we have an impossible fight on our hands. It therefore is no surprise that in surveying history, we read how people from time immemorial have complained of the mysterious riddles confronting them, and for which they could find no adequate answers.

Among the wide range of questions with which we have to cope every day, there are a few that have especially occupied human thinking.

Take the question of human origin, and the equally difficult problem of our ultimate destination. Where do we come from? Who really are the first human beings? What constitutes the end of life? What happens to our bodies when our lifeless remains are entrusted to the grave or are cremated? Is death final? Is there no more life after death? Or is death only a curtain that separates two life forms? Tell me, how do you or I know where we fit in here on earth?

The problem is that the minute we have started to reflect on this, right away new questions pop up screaming for answers with equal force. What ultimately is the purpose of life for us human beings here on earth? Do we have a task in this world, or is our existence no more than the flourishing of a flower, which blooms and then fades? Why are we here? Is there something like a calling, a task given us from above? And when we are at the end of life may we then peacefully die, confident that our life has been a blessing because our good deeds will follow us into eternity?

Even wondering about this is, at the same time, the onset of asking questions about the existence of the earth itself. Is the earth itself eternal? Will everything constructed by generations of humans – their cities, their ever-higher skyscrapers – will all that disappear because the world is destined to perish? If that is the case, why then fight the fight and expend the power when all is futile anyway?

Come to think of it, it really is quite unusual when all these questions arise in us. If they do, that is a great awakening; that is a great arousal jolting us out of the stupor of everyday life; that is a real revelation when we at last see life in all its marvelous mystery. It is then that the disguise now obscuring the real hurly-burly of our world is torn away, and all of a sudden we discover that our entire existence is veiled in enormous mysteries. Then we can only say: how strange that I am alive! It all starts with questions such as: Where do I originate? What actually is the purpose of my life? And when I pose these strange questions, then I am utterly amazed in my innermost being, and I smile in spite of being somewhat perplexed by the novelty of it all.

When all this started to germinate in you, you were perhaps lying somewhere in a meadow. Perhaps you were hearing the humming of honeybees, stretched out as you were amidst the multicolored field-flowers. Perhaps you studied the bizarre shapes of the cumulus clouds sailing across the immense blue sky. Perhaps you were sitting outside in the quietness of the night and leisurely looked up to the multitude of tiny light points, the faintly flickering stars, listening to the majestic melody of the nocturnal symphony. Then without warning there was a stirring in you, a strange emotion, a deep, rapturous sensation touching the core of life with all its strange, great questions. You have no idea where these thoughts came from, through which crevices they crept into the hidden corners of your soul. You wonder whether these feelings have always been there, now suddenly shaken awake. But now, fully conscious, they overwhelm you in an awesome amazement. You are flabbergasted that this strange being is you, and you don't know from where you came and how you came to be and for what reason you are here.

Until the very moment these thoughts penetrated into our consciousness, we only lived as in a dream. We then were just as lost in dreams as these white, sun-soaked clouds, sailing through the sky at the mercy of the wind. We were just as lost in dreams as the buzzing bees, seeking and humming and they don't know why. We were just as lost in dreams as the shining stars casting their glorious rays into the depth of the universe, not knowing why. In that same way our souls have dreamed, all those long years. They have thought, have coveted, have hated, have loved, have sought, have hoped, have cried, have feared. And now, suddenly, all this disappears, and here we are, confronted for the first time in our life with the awesome, mysterious riddle, the depth of all that is, the basis of all that is, the goal of all that is. Why, why? Why are things as they are? Where is the origin of everything and where does it end? What is the purpose of it all? And what place has that tiny spark that is my own fragile life in the totality of this all?

When the soul senses this, questions this, then our very innards are in uproar. There we stand before the very gates of the eternal truth, resembling a beggar, barefooted, draped in the threadbare rags of ignorance. And our soul knocks at the door of eternity, crying "O, God, if you exist, O, God, tell me what I am and why I am and why all is. I don't want to dream, my God, but I want to live and to live is to see. Show me your truth, your eternal truth, so that my soul may live! How has it come that I exist and that I do not see you? Why do these curtains, these heavy drapes, hang there between you and my soul, between my soul and the truth? Please, Lord: before the tiny spark of my life is extinguished in the global holocaust of dissolution, allow me first to see the origin of my life and my final destination."

Once we have started to look critically at the world, then we simply are trapped in the clutches of constantly new problems.

If there is a God, what is he like? Can we ever know him? How does he see us? Are we God too, or on the contrary, is God our great adversary, the ultimate destroyer?

And what are we ourselves? Are we really alive, or do we just imagine everything we think we experience? Do we have a body and a soul, or only a soul as some believe or only a body as others have supposed?

And what is it about the world around us? Does it really exist, or have I created it myself in my raving imagination, as in a dream I construct the strangest images in living color?

And what about this world? Can it really continue its present powerful urge for progress and development? Or is the opposite true – that it will slowly slide into oblivion? And this universe: How does it exist? How has it come into being, what sort of thinking is behind all of this? Is it a wonderfully, logically constructed entity, or is it one of a miraculous confusion, full of inconsistencies?

Tell me, do we have to obey certain laws in our life, ordinances on which we depend? Is there a moral order superseding everything in life? Are we capable of living according to that code? Do we have a will that can make decisions free from other influences? Or are we slaves chained to what surrounds us, a product of certain biological happenings? Suppose we are not obedient, are there certain punishments that force us to comply?

The trouble is, as soon as we even start to pose these questions, there is no longer an end. They leap at us, they cling to us, and demand answers. The only thing that we can do is to push them back, drown ourselves in the fast flow of life and even there discover that they lurk and threaten to pull us down.

Yes, I must admit, there is a lot of truth in that line by the poet De Genestet: "We humans wander on earth wrapped in riddles."

There are multitudes of men and women who hardly have any inkling – or interest – in these questions. They live their sedate and uneventful lives, and never give it a thought that they dwell in a world full of miracles. Their existence is a series of ups and downs, of enjoyment and hatred, of being happy and suffering, of struggling and respite, of being alive and facing death. Perhaps only at death's door does the ultimate question flash through their spirit:

What has been my life's purpose? Have I really pursued a goal? Is death the end, or . . . ? Did my life really make sense?

However, there are a tiny number of people who have become so captivated by finding answers to these questions that they cannot stop investigating them. They want to find out. They want to discover whether they truly are alive and the reason why. They are the ones who with every ounce of their thinking brain ponder the questions and have resolved that they want answers, before they can engage life to the full.

The very intention of this book is to briefly touch upon some of these cardinal problems, without scaring anybody, without sowing doubt. No, the sole purpose is to discover how to see and how to question.

After all, we do not seek as persons who despair. Our questioning is not an asking of the impossible. Believe me, there is a safe haven for our probing and pleading. God has spoken. The eternal mystery of the ultimate basis of everything that exists has been revealed. In Jesus Christ the Light has come, the Light that bans all darkness from our hearts and instills in us the unspeakable joy of having found and having been found.

All this reminds us of Jesus' profound words:

"I am the Way, the Truth, and the Life." Jesus Christ is the fulfillment of all our questions.

CHAPTER TWO

What Do We Know?

Above the entrance of the portal to scientific enterprise is chiseled the question: "What are we able to comprehend?" It is this question that is more important than any other. Why would we even start to discuss the ultimate questions when it can be clearly shown that these are completely beyond our intellectual capacity to grasp? If we were to do this we would resemble a young boy whose parents have given him a bow and arrow on his birthday and right away is busy aiming at the moon with the intention to shoot it down. In the same way we aim far too high when we start asking questions about God and about the purpose of the world when we have difficulty solving even the simplest problems.

What are we able to comprehend? It can also be put differently: What can we state with complete certainty? Where is the basis, the ultimate foundation, of our knowing? At what exact moment can we state that this or that is beyond doubt, because it is totally trustworthy? And when we have arrived at that conclusion, then, at the same time, we are at the start of a most difficult journey. Why? Because then we are faced with the question how we, departing from this single focal point, can arrive at an answer to all other questions. This can be compared to a hive from which bees buzz away in all different directions, but always return to their fixed base.

In the course of the ages there has been more than one answer to where exactly this fixed point is, and where the boundaries are beyond which we may question our uncertainty.

The simplest, the most child-like answer is this: we know what we see with our own eyes because in seeing we observe the necessary truth. Once we have seen things ourselves, then all doubt disappears. There are people who even have the audacity to reverse this proposition by confessing: if I can't see it, then I don't believe it. If I only had even a glimpse of God, then all my doubts about him would disappear. It simply is impossible for me to believe in a Higher Being that is invisible. Direct observation is the strongest proof of knowledge.

I have intentionally labeled this answer "child-like." It is understandable that initially some find this satisfactory, but on second thought they will have to admit that this opinion cannot be maintained.

Does a person really fathom what she sees? Say that you observe the rising of the moon. At that point it looks far larger than when it is high up in the dark sky. So that really proves nothing. When do you see the moon as it really is?

Suppose you look at the mountains. From far away they look blue. Are they really that color? When you come closer they show a multitude of hues. Or if you look into a deep well the bottom seems to be much narrower, yet overall it has the same width. So what the eye registers is not what really goes on. Or take the blue sky, which looks like a gigantic dome resting on the earth, like a tent, and yet it is quite simple to show that reality is totally different. The same is true of the stars. They look like tiny blips on a high, high vault. Do you believe what you see or do you believe what we are told – that the stars are far larger than our world? We see the trees as green and blood as red, the ripe grain as yellow and the sky as blue. Do you know that there are people who see these colors totally differently, who cannot see the distinction between red and green? Of course they are colorblind, you say. But don't they have the right to maintain that there may be something wrong with *your* eyes? Who can guarantee that your vision is the correct one?

So you think you see the world as it really is. Let's assume you are right. In a dream you too believe what you observe, such as strange happenings and queer animals. Can you prove that you never did dream but what you now see is verily, verily the truth? Isn't it just as well possible that you now are dreaming and that you perhaps are dreaming that you are awake? How can we prove that this is not the case?

And what perhaps clinches the argument is this thought, that precisely what really matters in life is something that is beyond our viewing range. We can't see the love of a mother, nor can we detect the thoughts arising in our soul. We simply cannot see the images, the desires, the thought patterns agitating in our brains, nor can we pinpoint the life that stirs in our blood, in our heart, and in our psyche. We can't deny that these matters are real. Are those not exactly the issues that are of the most importance? These invisible matters – life, the thinking process, love – are they not precisely the issues that build the world and shape it? How then can we assume that only what is visible is guaranteed?

We have to go in a different direction because we really don't know what we see. It is highly possible that something of which I am certain appears later to be not true at all. Thus seeing does not eliminate doubt, for the question remains whether we have made the correct observation, or whether we have imagined seeing it and whether all this has really been true. Seeing alone is not the ultimate criterion, does not touch the heart of the matter, the starting point from which we can set out to explore the different avenues open to us. In other words, we must continue to search for definite answers. It is possible that there are persons who do have the correct answer. There must be a way out, because we know what we know and we know what we think. The thinking process is the absolute guarantee we need. If something is really logical, if something is irrefutably true, then we have arrived at the stage where doubt is eliminated.

The fact is, nobody will deny the statement that 2 + 2 equals 4, or that 7 + 8 gives the sum of 15. Nobody will dispute you when you say that the surface area of a triangle is equal to half its height times the base or that the sum of its three corners is 180 degrees. We assume that what we can positively prove is something that is unconditionally true, something we can rely on one hundred percent.

At first glance this assumption is completely acceptable. When pure observation may not give the ultimate proof, perhaps pure reason, the thinking process, will manage to bridge the gap and finally provide us with the desired outcome.

Yet it is not difficult to demonstrate that this too is not the final solution. After all, our reasoning too needs a certain starting point. We simply cannot begin a thought without having a structural framework. And it is exactly there where the trouble starts: Where do we locate such a point of departure? From where do we begin our wanderings?

In mathematics we start with assuming certain unproved propositions, which then are considered true. If that is the case, then the rest is also beyond dispute. But nobody can with the utmost certainty claim that they, indeed, are true, that they are beyond any dispute.

Some have said that we yet have one single fixed truth, and that is that we our sure of our own existence. I exist, and I know this beyond a shadow of a doubt. From there I simply may proceed in the assumption that I cannot possibly make an error. Others, however, have started their point of departure in the existence of God. God exists, and using that assumption we may continue our thinking process. What does that involve? Where do we go from there, and where do we end up? Doesn't there always remain a gnawing doubt whether that too may turn out to be not true? And if that is the case, then the entire structure will turn out to be based on an untruth. That's why even our thinking may turn out to be insufficient when complete certainty is at stake.

In the end the question remains: What can we know for sure? To that question we must return time and again. Do we have a fixed truth from which we can start? If we have that, then perhaps we can proceed, because from that single certain point we can arrive at the ultimate truth. But to get there is very difficult, and also a really painful procedure.

Above the entrance of the portal to scientific enterprise is chiseled the question: "What do we really know?"

What is our answer? Perhaps we have to admit: I know one thing for sure: I really know nothing. If that is the case, then that really implies that we no longer can proceed with our enquiry. If we know nothing, how then can we look for answers to the burning, heartfelt questions?

Where is the fixed base of our knowledge? At what point can we say: here I stand assured, here is no longer any doubt whatsoever?

CHAPTER THREE

Faith

The decades in which we are living have been periods of amazing progress in human knowledge. It is indeed utterly remarkable how far and wide science has expanded in every field. It is not only that we daily experience the fruits of the flourishing of all branches of science, the technical advances in the medical field, but we also have gained a greater insight into history, into nature, and especially into the field of astronomy, an ever-deeper penetration into the ever-more mysterious universe. It is undoubtedly true that we have made amazing advances in all fields. In our laboratories we do experiments never before imagined. Our insight everywhere has been deepened and widened. All this we can state with immense gratitude. It is totally understandable that people today delight in these scientific accomplishments; that they observe all this with the utmost satisfaction and proudly observe how the body of knowledge, to which thousands of intelligent men and women from everywhere in the world contribute, grows by the day.

And yet, there is no ground at all for pride and for self-satisfaction. There are — as there have been throughout history — those who with a certain anxiety view these developments and have come to the disappointing conclusion that, in the final analysis, we really know very little.

Of course the question arises: How is that possible? How can these two situations exist simultaneously? We know so much and yet we know so little. Do we then have both reason to rejoice and a ground for humility? That seems to be the situation.

This dilemma is easy to explain for two reasons. In the first place we can immediately state that, with all our knowledge, we still do not understand the essence of the matter, because in the end we always encounter the mystery. We sense this as soon as we start to look deeper into the ultimate questions.

We are aware; we are conscious and know what goes on in the world and what motivates us. But don't ask what consciousness is, where it originates, where it is based. What does that mean, "to be conscious"? How come that at night, during sleep, it goes away, but in the morning when we wake up, it is part of us again? What does that mean? Also, what is the human will, or character? What is my "I"? It's really discouraging when we pause for a while and meditate on this. Indeed, we are in every way to ourselves a confounding enigma, a mysterious riddle.

Here I don't even touch upon that incomprehensible mystery of how it is possible that bodily symptoms, and actions in our nervous system, translate into psychical phenomena. For instance: the nerves in my eye experience a certain sensation, and at once I become aware that somewhere out there is a ray of light. This is one of the most miraculous of all transformations: the change from the material to something psychical. This is so immensely mysterious that it is far beyond the human capacity to acquire the needed knowledge to explain this. It's really sad for us people, immersed in so much scholarship, that we haven't got the faintest idea how an occurrence that happens every moment of the day, even at this instant, cannot be fathomed.

Or give a thought to something such as the question "What is life?" I don't mean whether you can analyze this phenomenon, are able to describe it, but whether you understand something of the riddle that roams in being human, the something that makes a person different from everything else that has no life. Or give a thought to trying to understand what takes place in a man or woman, in an animal or a plant, the moment they die? What is life itself, where does it come from? Tell me what happens when life reveals itself in these phenomena.

The questions multiply. What is electricity, what is matter? We have split the atom, and within its confines discovered new worlds. Do we know what they are, have we understood the building blocks of the universe and where they originate? Have we grasped the secret of magnetism – that marvelous entity by which proton and electron keep each other in balance through positive and negative electricity, the force that holds the atom in check and so keeps the universe from falling apart? What really are the laws of nature, the forces that keep the world from imploding? Where is their basis? What actually are they anyway?

You really don't have to be a miserable pessimist to see that in reality we understand only a tiny, tiny bit of that massive cosmic structure in which we live, and that we perhaps never will fathom it completely. We do know the symptoms, we are able to trace the laws regulating these phenomena; but looking behind the scenes, penetrating to the essence of the matter, we are unable to do. We even fail to understand ourselves or others for that matter; we don't know what death is or life, spirit or matter, plant or animal: in short, we fumble forever in mysteries. But really that does not matter at all, and all this is nothing to be ashamed of, provided we admit this and humbly recognize our ignorance.

In addition to all this there is also another matter that forces us even more to abandon our pretentions. We humans may claim to know a lot, but one thing escapes us: the road to profound and true happiness. Just as scientific knowledge grows step by step, in the same way we also become more and more aware of that vacuum in us, the lack of genuine contentment. In the last few decades the world around us has experienced tensions and unrest as never before. Everywhere in the world people are perplexed and anxious about the future. They experience the present planetary turmoil and the disasters that sooner or later will affect them all, frightening even the most stouthearted. The prospect that our war against the planet will rage on into perpetuity and that peace has become an impossibility gives us a feeling of fear and disquiet. Our tremendous technical capability seems to be more a curse than a blessing because morally we are not sufficiently strong to combat these developments. Everything that is invented today is used tomorrow to destroy and exterminate. In many ways humanity resembles a child that unfortunately has acquired a weapon that is beyond its capacity to correctly control.

I believe we are faced here with the frightening aspect of our own powerlessness and ignorance. We simply are not capable of changing ourselves and our fellow humans. We simply don't know how we can change our nature. We all sense that our world is on the road to horrific chaos and there is not a single person who can tell us how to extract ourselves from this mess. We know a lot, we are capable of doing much, but the possibility of changing ourselves and our world so that we may experience shalom, is beyond our capacity. It appears that by powerful, invisible forces we are pushed to pursue a path of expanding knowledge and increasing capacity, while simultaneously it is becoming more evident all the time that this road will only lead to immeasurable misery because we humans simply cannot change. Egoism without destructive intent is sin nevertheless, but in itself not harmful. However, that same egoism becomes a lethal force when armed with destructive capacity. Hate without dangerous weapons is still sin, but not fatal. Hatred armed to the teeth is capable of creating hell on earth. Every step we take to increase our technical know-how can lead to endless disaster as long as we do not have a change of heart.

We humans are at the threshold of limits that we cannot cross. Our knowing is drowning in the ocean of mystery. Our ability to act is limited by the lack of willpower preventing us from discovering the road to a true change of lifestyle.

It is possible that these discoveries will affect the human mind, bringing on a deep depression unless we live in the faith that there is a Higher Power who rules our life. Faith is the sole source that can make us safe and secure and can open vistas enabling us to invigorate our life.

It is one of the remarkable human traits that we all at birth are endowed with a steadfast faith that the world in which we live makes eminent sense. When a newborn child starts to breathe, it does this instinctively, trusting that the surrounding air is composed of the right amount of oxygen and the correct measures of other ingredients suitable for our lungs to function at maximum capacity. The very first act a new human being does is based on the faith that nobody has fooled around with the air and that we exist in a world that functions within properly set norms. When I look around me and see what happens out there I do this in full confidence that my eyes do not betray me, that they have been so adjusted to the light that they provide me with an image of what takes place out there. When I ponder the questions of the world as I perceive it, I do this in the inexpressible silence of my faith that my thoughts run parallel with thoughts of the great Thinker whose image is reflected in this world. A small child who with every step asks his parents why everything is as it is, does this, without being aware of this, based on the instinctive assumption that everything in the world is there for a reason. That apple trees have blossoms is not an accident; that butterflies look for flowers is not a freak happening: all this makes sense and is done for a reason. This is the very foundation of our faith. When we grow older there may come a time when we may doubt the rationality of our existence, questioning whether our life is senseless and without purpose, yet in spite of that in our innermost being our confidence remains unaffected. Every heartbeat, every breath we take, is confirmation that an invisible, rational Power has ordered our life in conjunction with the world around us.

When we inquire after the source of our knowledge, we can never simply discard that faith. Why would I rely on my eyes and ears if I did not believe that One greater than I has fashioned my eye and ear, geared to the world that surrounds me? Why would I rely on my own thinking if I did not believe that One wiser than I has ordered my thoughts in such a way that it corresponds with the order he himself has laid down in this world? How would I dare to or be able to live if I did not at every moment abide in the faith that there must be an invisible Power who carries and directs my little life in the greater context of all things? I simply must trust that I am not an object of some game, must realize that there is no foul play here. Only based in faith is life possible.

This is not the last word regarding faith. We will come back to this. When we approach the questions of redemption, then we automatically touch again upon the matter of faith but then in a totally different sense. Then our attention will be focused on the words in the Bible: "believe in the Lord Jesus and you will be saved." Then again we will deal with faith, but that is a different matter. We now are still busy contemplating the very foundations of all knowing and understanding. In these fields we too have to deal with the requirement of faith. We can in good conscience assume that our eyes and our ears, our brains and our reason can lead us to the truth . . . provided we assume that we have been created on this world, and that we fit here perfectly. When that is the case, then there is no reason not to proceed.

There is another way to express all this, and that is by relying on what we know so that we may joyfully keep on plugging, provided we begin to believe that we are part of a rational universe, and thus assume that this world makes sense where each part fits in with the other, where the eye relates to the visible and the ear is geared to the audible. When in that way everything fits and makes sense, then indeed we are secure. But this thesis, in the final analysis, can only be maintained when we confess that an almighty and all-wise God has created the world and the human race in mutual dependence. Faith in God also means faith in the world. Forget about God and gone is the guarantee that all of life is not a pure piece of fraud, an awesome act of bewitching.

There's where faith comes in. After all, in the final analysis all science is based on faith. The tiny vessel of our human knowledge can only safely float in the currents of doubt when she is anchored in the faith that we dwell in a rational, sensible world, fashioned by the One who in infinite wisdom formed everything in harmonious relationship to everything else. Believe and you will live!

CHAPTER FOUR

The World Order

When we look around us into the whole wide world out there, we immediately are overwhelmed by the rich diversity we see everywhere. The immense richness is simply astounding. The abundance of varieties of beings and the many kinds of creatures is beyond belief. A closer survey discovers ever-newer shapes and forms and daily encounters with different, previously unknown species.

However, once we have more closely examined what goes on around us, then instead of mere admiration for the amazing newness of it all, we are struck even more by the unity and order that are evident everywhere, because everything on earth is somehow harmoniously connected to everything else. The one species influences the other and the one creature depends on the other. Plants cannot exist without the earth that feeds them. Animals, on the other hand, cannot function without plants, as these are often the sole source for their food.

The phenomena of day and night, of summer and winter, of rain and drought, of heat and cold, all are part of the grand chain of happenings, depending on where the sun happens to be and from where the wind blows. The one event influences another and yet the one cannot exist without the presence of the other.

By further investigation we discover that the order is one full of purpose. The great connectedness of all these entities is at the same time the reason why the totality is served by it as well. We don't even need to explore everything too deeply to discover the amazing fact that behind everything there is an invisible set of laws: that the one as it were serves to complete the other. The butterflies serve the flowers just as much as the flowers serve the butterflies. The sun, that big, beneficial celestial body, which from an immeasurable distance bathes the earth in multicolored splendor, is itself not conscious that from a distance of millions of miles it brings light and warmth. It is the sun that maintains life on earth. It is the sun that causes plants to sprout out of the moist earth. It is the sun that removes mourning and remakes it into merriment. If the sun had a mind of its own, then perhaps it would muse: I shine because that's my nature; I delight in it; it's the joy of my life. But it knows not that a Hand mightier than the sun has included it in the beautiful law of serving. Because, unknowingly, that so superior sun serves the tiny, tiny plant that full of life expectancy courageously stretches its stem to absorb its rays.

That little plant cannot think beyond its nature. It winks at the sun and dreams of the joy that awaits it in a life of light and sunshine. But it has no inkling that it serves just as much as it is served by others. It serves the minuscule seeds it now carries and that later will form new plants. It serves the animal, looking for food, or is needed to help another plant using it as a crutch to climb higher. In manifold ways it serves other creatures that need support or shade or nourishment or moisture.

When we look around us with open eyes and minds, then there is one thing that time and again touches us to the core: it's all about serving. The law of serving is at the heart of every creature: it is the overarching purpose for every being. That law makes it possible for the entire world to exist. Every creature may think that it is there only for itself, but in the final analysis it is nothing else but a servant for others. To be alive, to exist at all, finds its destination simply in serving others. Without that law nothing else can be.

Yet that law of serving is remarkable in more than one way. What is so truly amazing is that, as a rule, no creature is there for the sole reason of serving, as they all think that self-help is their sole goal, but all that serving goes automatically, and thus is simply an unconscious act. It is as if a mighty hand brings all this into motion and, in spite of itself, stimulates this selfless serving. This serving, therefore, is not a sacrifice, is not a duty, but an in-born act, without compulsion, without intent. Each single being is there according to its nature, but everything together is so oriented that the existence of the one supports the other and maintains it.

In the second place, it soon becomes clear that the act of serving changes in direct proportion to the higher status of the species. There appear to be three categories of beings in creation, three large classes, which differ among themselves.

The first class consists of the ordinary, lifeless material. That too involves service, but it is one that is ostensibly accidental. The fertile soil serves the tiny seeds that germinate there but they are unaware of this, and that's alright with them. A blanket of snow, with its dense cover, serves to protect the field against the bitter cold. The high mountains also serve when they gather the snow in the winter and preserve it throughout the spring only to release it in the summer and so replenish the rivers with their pure and cool water. But all this proceeds unknowingly. Then there is the rotating of the earth around its axis. Is this not also a serving of immense meaning because this daily motion makes the transition from day to night possible, something that, in the final analysis, enables us to live? All these elements are unaware of their serving. Sometimes, circumstances may cause severe damage. This happens, for instance, when unusual rainfall results in widespread flooding, or when a merciless sun burns the promising harvest to a crisp. In the seemingly nonliving world the great order of natural law still rules, generally attuned to the great law of service; but under the prodding of the great Adversary it is now more and more inclined toward destruction.

In the second place another broad range of species can be found in the smaller of the animals and plants. In that segment service takes on a more defined role, has more purpose, more unity, and looks to be more intentional. The plant offers itself with all its tender organs, and, when circumstances become unfavorable, it even changes its approach to other methods to serve better. Upon closer examination it appears that the typical plant is less concerned about its own welfare and more about the well-being of its progeny.

The mother offers her life to advance that of her child. The full ear shrivels to dust when the seeds have been released into the earth. To propagate the line the single specimen makes the ultimate sacrifice. The mother protects the young against all danger and would rather perish than neglect her newborn. There also is evidence of a peculiar "specimen-egoism." The one specimen often lives at the expense of the other, annihilates the other. But whatever is the case, in these particular sorts of beings service is more delineated; the single specimen serves the body, the single entity serves the species, the mother serves the child. All damaging influences are avoided, and if that proves impossible, then some accommodation is sought. In that case the most favorable options are pursued, especially for the young as they often need all the care possible. Then the act of serving acquires a real purpose, when, in that entire living world, there is only one object, one goal that supersedes all other functions.

At the very top of these three categories is the final stage, that of the conscious possessors of free will, the human species.

With humans service is simply different, is infinitely richer, but because of that also more difficult. It is self-evident that the aforementioned natural instincts are also present in the human race. There too the care for children; there too a touch of "specimen-egoism." But these powerful instinctive forces are here recognized as such. Humans know exactly what they do and why they do it.

Consequently humans have much greater opportunity to serve. Every category in society serves the other; a world can't do without medical doctors, but it also needs carpenters and farmers. Service becomes specialized as each assumes a small part of the great societal task.

The trouble with us humans is that the inclination to only serve our specific needs is both stronger and more dangerous, promoting our welfare at the expense of our fellow citizens. Even though we are more conscious of what we do and are able to gauge the needs of others, we also can easily ignore the plight of our neighbors. That happens all too easily when we center life around our own interests, while often pushing away the needs of others. In short: serving is for most of us something we are loath to do, as we are driven by egoism, the "I come first" instinct. That "I come first" inclination often overwhelms all other feelings, stifles them, and comes out on top. With us humans the urge of "me first" usually takes priority over conflict, the struggle, the concept of serving.

Given this weakness, we humans have been given a command: serve one another! This serving, something all other species of the world accomplish automatically and by instinct, we humans have to implement in full awareness of what we do. In this third category we are given the command, the moral code: Love your neighbor as yourself.

There has been one, the human Jesus Christ, who has expressed his life's calling: The Son of Man, Humanity personified, has not come to be served, but to serve.

CHAPTER FIVE

Where Do We Come From?

Only now can we elaborate on the age-old and immense question dealing with the origin of all things, that controversial topic: "Where do we come from?"

In the foregoing, two matters became quite clear: in the first place, all our knowledge and understanding is relative, indicated by the imperfection and the basic faith-assumption of all our scientific endeavors. In the second place, we have seen that the world can only be understood as a holistic entity where every single member is there to serve the other. The basic law for humanity, the world's constitution, so to say, is the law of serving: on it rests the foundation of the entire planet.

Thus when we turn to the question "what is the origin of it all?" we must as much as possible profit from what we have discussed so far. We must guard against falling for hard-and-fast answers because in reality we stand before the gate of knowledge lacking access to definite solutions. We have to look elsewhere for such a starting point, something that will give us a decisive affirmation to the law of service. The notion that everything happened by accident is not a possibility I want to accept.

Where do we come from? Innumerable generations have wrestled with this problem and constantly argued over it. Where does the radiant sun come from, the source behind all that powers life? From where are these treasures of diversity in humans and animals? Of course, we can say that this is none of our business: we are here and that is enough. Yet it is clear that the question "from where?" must be answered, because it is of the utmost importance and key to many other questions that we also must pose.

From where art thou, human? Is it God's Hand that fashioned thee?

To be more direct: Do we carry traces of his divine wisdom and omnipotence? Or has the great power of Fate, over the millions of years, led us to what we are? If it is the former, then we are subject to the divine law, but that also implies that we are the object of divine care; we are not a link in the chain of higher evolution, but the crown, the ultimate accomplishment of a marvelous act of creation. But if it is the latter, we are at a crossroad, caught between darkness behind us and darkness in front of us; there is no essential norm, no essential care, no essential purpose, no essential direction.

In connection with this difficult question, logic alone can hardly be the deciding factor. Our intellectual grasp can, to some extent, understand the state of the world as it is now, but the long period of history can only be reconstructed with a great degree of uncertainty. That's why insignificant indications are often accepted as definite proof and offered as valid explanations.

Here, more than ever, we must use the concept of probability. Caution is the key. Our approach should be to state: it could well be possible that this is the case, but we cannot exclude the option that everything is just the opposite. Such ambiguity is the only way to proceed.

However, there are several indications that point to a divine origin of creation. First of all there is the immense differentiation that endlessly amazes us. Why is everything in the world so geared to the law of serving? Why is it that all things fit together like clockwork and complement each other? Each creature exists for its own sake and is convinced that it only serves and enriches itself, and yet, it is at the same time a collaborator in the functioning of the totality of the universe. When we observe the order in the natural world, then we can only conclude that a Superior Thinking Power has formed everything. This becomes more and more evident as we penetrate deeper and deeper into the world. Science, which in the last hundred years has made conquest after conquest, always proceeds from the assumption that it all comes forth from well-planned design. This presumption is time and again confirmed with every new discovery. The majestic thinking process, the utter logic of it all, has penetrated every aspect of the grandiose creation. It is especially there where the image of the omniscient God is revealed.

A second indication is this: it is nearly impossible to imagine that the world has come forth from itself. That's why creation deniers prefer to say that the entire matter is shrouded in uncertainty. But it is certain that incalculable quantities of energy are available out there. The sun, for instance, has for eons radiated its vast supply of energy into the solar system. Such immense accumulations cannot simply be seen as being purely accidental. Actually in nature it always is precisely the other way around. Usually these energy sources are spread evenly, avoiding large concentrations. That is just another reason why a chance evolvement of the universe is so difficult to accept.

Another reason: we often encounter inexplicable events. It is true that much makes sense when we combine the basic elements in nature with the laws of nature, yet these very fundamental elements and these very natural laws defy explanation. When we analyze all these and scrutinize every chemical compound, we are still faced with questions such as "What are they?," "Where do they come from, and how?," and "Why is this the case?"

Then there still is the matter of natural laws. In the last few decades scientific research has explored and altered its position regarding the concept of natural law, with the result that the questions simply have multiplied and the mystery has become even more pronounced.

Closer examination often ends up magnifying the mystery, often leads to an abyss so steep that no human thinking can fathom its depth.

It stands to reason that these three points in themselves are not totally convincing. Mathematical rationalities have, I must admit, a certain compelling proving power, but when we deal with the overarching, life-dominating questions, then reason is relegated to a minor role. This is because we humans, when we delve deeper into these problems, are far too personally involved. When our entire life has become estranged from God, when we purposely have pulled away from the power of God's majesty, then it seems that a kind of blindness darkens our mind, and it is as if our eyes no longer can tolerate the brilliance of his glory. Our thinking is far less objective and unprejudiced than we ourselves imagine. When we look around us and listen to people's opinions in these days of global turmoil, then we immediately notice that often, trying to grasp the problems, we believe what we want to believe. Our understanding and our intellect follow what our heart tells us to think. In the same way, but much more so, this also applies to the all-important questions regarding God and the world. This is why the wind-vane of our thinking registers remarkable variations. To be cognizant of the truth is primarily a moral given and only granted to the pure of heart. A life lived for sensual desires, in hate and with monetary ambition, robs us of insight into the deepest realities on which the universe is founded.

In other words: concerning the all-important question of the origin of all things our intellect, our human logic, cannot possibly be the final arbiter. Those who want to wait until scientific studies have pronounced the final verdict must wait till the end of days. Here we humans are faced with the final choice from which we cannot escape. We humans are like a child, a foundling, abandoned by its parents, who later in life can never with certainty state from where it came.

The Christian faith, realizing this truth, strongly stresses the confession: I believe in God, the Father, creator of heaven and earth. That is not a scientific conclusion, not a well-rounded statement, but it rests on faith in God's Word. When I, in this world, amidst an untold number of mysteries, ponder the question of "Where do we originate?" I only can trust that the whole of this rational and yet so mysterious universe has been wrought by a superior Reason, by an all-wise Maker who also is our Father.

Regarding this creation, it simply is a mighty divine deed. In the final analysis we don't have a clue what has been there before. When the Bible touches on this it always does so in terms of enigmatic depth. It reminds me of these beautiful words of Psalm 33:9: "For God spoke and it came to be; he commanded and it stood firm" (NIV). After the words "God spoke" we tend to pause, holding our breath, wondering what comes next, and then the magical words follow: "and it came to be." A New Testament text comes to mind: "What is seen was not made out of what was visible" (Hebrews 11:3 NIV). These are just a few feeble indications of the inexpressible mystery by which we understand the concept of "creation." Through his almighty will God brought the world into being. Then the stars and the planets took their ever-rotating places in the infinite heavens. Then the Milky Way weaved its way as a radiating ring around our starry sky. Then our earth, this tiny earth, started her royal road. And just as this planet always revolves around the sun, striding, as it were, in the glow originating from that solar source, so this universe exists only in the light that flows from the face of the eternal. He is the Sun of the world; out of him and through him and to him everything is.

One of the great possibilities behind God's creation is that he did not shape this world as a completely finished entity. I have no idea what the world looked like when God encountered this unformed mass. Perhaps the dim and dark and dense nothingness was first boiling and roiling chaos. Perhaps this undefined cauldron was first seething with all-consuming ferocity. Yet out of this quivering and billowing mass, mountains emerged, pushed from the very innards of the earth with irrepressible force. Like a newborn baby, shaking and shivering, the dark world rose up.

Soon after that, through the will of the almighty, the Creator, the first signs of life sprouted forth. Plants started to grow on the mountain slopes, in the crevices here and on the boundless steppes there. And so the grand process of creation was perfected: the song of the genesis of all things, the melody of wisdom and power. As the last of all visible creatures, humanity appeared. They are the most dependent of all beings, needing air to breathe, food in a variety of forms and substances to stay alive. They only could enter into their worldly home when all other creatures were there already. They never could be the beginning: they could only be the end of it all. Their hearts mirrored the glow of eternity.

It is in this way that the Bible allows us a glimpse into the origin of all matter, including the origin of our very being.

CHAPTER SIX

Who Are We?

Somewhere in the Bible, in a rather obscure location, is a description of Adam. It is a wonderful term: the son of God. And, in essence, that also is the answer to the question we posed. Who are we? We are sons and daughters of God. It's as simple as that: we are God's children, born from the eternal light.

We can have all sorts of opinions regarding the essence of being human. We can state that we are the end product of the agitation of the powers of nature. We are here thanks to an evolution process out of which we have slowly emerged, originating from lower creatures that have had the capability to become creatures of a higher order. On the other hand we also can state that the human being in essence is "the child of God." This statement also does not mean that humans somehow at one time fell out of the sky, but it does mean that human beings, even though they are in their bodily forms related to the animals, are and remain "dust." At the same time we humans are totally different from animals. We have something in us that is unmistakably noble, something that cannot be explained in any other way. We carry a magnificent crown, in the form of a mysterious treasure that guides us, as a compass, in all our life's happenings, which has caused us to rise far beyond the world of animals.

Again the choice between these two visions of life can never be made by reason alone. Our brains can come up with many arguments for one of these opinions. Our power of understanding can clearly and decisively show that we humans are mere dust, after all, or, on the other hand, emphasize that humans possess a power far exceeding perishable matter, but ultimately the choice never really depends on our cognitive faculties alone. What is our opinion about us, ourselves? Who do we say we are?

To all this I must add a word of caution: the heart is not really without prejudice. After all, if we state that humans have their origin in animals and that we, in the final analysis, must be regarded as highly developed members of that classification, then, indeed, we can be excused when we so often behave like animals. Why should we be surprised when we humans, during wartime, are eager to shed blood and incarcerate and gas millions? Why should we be surprised when we, like animals, are consumed by our passions? Looking at human behavior, is it really not amazing that we have progressed so far on the road to becoming more human? Is it really not surprising that, in many ways, we have advanced to being more dignified? Even though we are still far from perfection, even though we still face a long road, there is no reason to be discouraged. The twilight in which we live is not the setting of the day, but the dawn of a new day. But is that really the case?

Yes, says Friedrich Nietzsche, the man who proclaimed the gospel of the Übermensch, the so-called perfect human. He has been the eloquent prophet predicting the arrival of such an ideal person. A human being, so said he, is a person who as yet has to be conquered, by pointing the road to the Human-King. We humans are the living bridge between the animal and the Human-King. As yet we are not the end product, but a link on a long road to perfection. That's why he urges us to be full of hope and confidence when we walk on the road of evolution.

On the other hand, when we believe that we are God's children, that we, unlike all other creatures, have, from our very inception, been of royal descent, then at the same time we must also acknowledge our fall into sin, still for us a daily occurrence. It is the sorry truth that the level of our life remains far below the standard we should have as true human beings. Perhaps in our best moments we approach this state when we let go of the world and reach to the sky, and sense something of what true living is all about. Why is it that in our day-to-day existence we run around in circles, simply going nowhere, being prone to push others away in our quest for self-promotion?

Why do we, all of us, worshipfully bow down before our own holy "I"? And yet we sense that we, by doing so, act foolishly, that a state of self-sacrifice offers much more promise and, in the final analysis, creates a much happier life than one that only pursues self-interest. All this is so difficult that it is almost impossible to act differently. At times, when we grow older, it might go through our mind that we could have done so much more with the gifts we had. Isn't it true that our life is mostly one of monotony and dullness? Why? Because looking deep into ourselves, we realize that we are prone to turn away from God, keep him behind a wall, hide away from him, refuse to let him speak to us, stifle the spirit in us. We are, we must admit, fallen children of God, backing away from him all the time.

That we are indeed of high origin can be traced to three components.

The first feature is that we are moral beings. We sense the difference between good and evil. It is true that we hardly ever live up to that claim, but nevertheless, just about everybody has a faint notion that there are certain norms. Our life, our thoughts, our conversations, they all are subject to a higher law. We are aware of evil that cannot be tolerated, requiring punishment, calling for judgment. On the other hand there is good, there is virtue, for which we must aim, which we must welcome, and for which we deserve praise. In the conflict between these two moral forces we, with heart and soul, must side with the good. That moral good requires of us that we never give a thought to do otherwise, that we unambiguously surrender to its ruling power. This phenomenon is so remarkable that all nations are touched by this good, that everywhere, to the amazement of all, a moral code is adopted, which serves in us as a mysterious compass to guide us. Yes, there is no doubt that the ideal of holiness is something still present in all of us.

In the second place we have an innate urge to learn. Of course we want to get ahead in the world, but that does not mean that we forget about the world's problems, and, especially today, the care for creation. Already the nations of antiquity had acquired deep knowledge of the heavens, of the course of the stars and planets, and profoundly pondered the origin of it all and investigated their own place in society. The quest for what takes place around us keeps our minds occupied all the time: in that sense we are like children who always ask why. We all are searchers, looking for unity, for harmony, for the essence and the destination of creation. It is as if we want to pierce through creation as if it were a piece of polished crystal, in our desire to discover the origin of everything. It is as if our heartfelt desire is to find that pure fragment of knowledge so that we can solve all our problems and create an all-encompassing unity.

The third characteristic is our historic desire to live in harmony, in community, and in peace with the divine will. Here too it is not difficult to cite many examples from tribes and regions everywhere as proof of this statement. Isn't it true that people have always offered the best they had to their deities, because they desired peace with the higher powers, acknowledging them as entities rising above the secular? There is an inclination in our hearts too that rises above the plain worldly; a desire that urges us to seek solitude so that we can listen in all quietness to God's voice, that almost silent whispering that faintly echoes throughout the universe. Our urge to reenter the sphere divine, our desire to escape the vortex of worldly forces and to be reunited in communion with God, is one of the essential elements that have dominated history. It is as if we all, in our innermost being, picture an ideal form of justice, encompassing the harmony and the communion with the Origin of all things.

In these three components, we, as humans, are at the zenith of all beings. That's why we are creatures of a different order and why our history is one of entirely different forces.

However, these three significant features are not within the human grasp. We crave them, we fervently long for them; and exactly this deep desire is proof positive that these longed-for traits are part and parcel of our being, something we desperately want to acquire. They form an essential part of our makeup; they are our own crown, they determine our royal status. They are the aspects that determine our royal descent: we are born of God. We are Adam . . . God's children.

CHAPTER SEVEN

The Meaning of Life

One of the most frequently asked questions nowadays is "What is life's meaning?," a question that, given the time we live in, is highly understandable. Just look at our own life. We live a limited number of years. Let me take a high age, say ninety years, yet in these ninety years there have been only a few instances in which we truly lived to the full. We dwell only a few years as toddler and pre-teen. We sometimes experience real life in our teens when for the first time falling in love shakes our innermost being and it seems that then our entire existence is on edge. But that too passes and life goes on as in a sleep. Once in a while we are shaken awake when world-shocking events reach even our comfortable position, but those things happen only sporadically. For the major part of our life we just dream on, which means that we get caught up in the routine of daily living: we come home, we eat, we drink, we read a bit or listen to the radio, and then off to bed. For some there is a promotion at work, a bit of extra pay; our kids grow up, go to school, get settled, and we ourselves grow old. Even though times have changed, for most people this is how life evolves. Emotionally, we sometimes are a bit down, we sometimes feel happy, but never to the extreme. We sometimes love others, and at times we hate people, but we never overdo it. We express agreement, we find something boring, we laugh, we cry, but in all this we never get too deeply involved. We hardly ever are shaken to the core, to the extent that our total being is involved. In short, quietly and dutifully we continue to travel on the monotonous path that has been the way with most people. We grow old and we die.

The above describes life for most of us in the Western world. A life quite uncomplicated, and not without merit, I must add; but the question remains whether a life such as this has any merit at all. We could say that it is like a dream, a good dream or a bad one, depending on one's choice. We could even suggest that it is a performance, a comedy or a tragedy, depending on one's opinion. But the recurring question is whether it has any meaning, whether it makes sense, whether it is worth the effort. Does it have a larger significance? Here we come to the core of the matter, touch upon the burning question of our day.

And actually it is not at all surprising that these questions emerge exactly now in our time. Our age is the age of the machine. In the Middle Ages the labor of the individual still carried a personal touch: he or she could perhaps devote life to a *métier*. Life then occurred in slow motion and was often hard and difficult, but the final product showed the individual's talents and hallmark. Compare this to the millions of workers today who either are stuck in a repetitious assembly line or have no work at all, many dropping out of the working force because machines have eliminated their position. The question is: What is the meaning of such a life? What should such a person feel about his life when he has reached the end of his days? What has he or she accomplished? What was his or her contribution to the world?

Until now we were a valuable and still a necessary extension of the machine. It is no wonder, in our age of the elimination of much meaningful work, that, with ever-greater insistence, the call arises: What is the sense of it all? What is the meaning of life? I know we go to bat for our lives, try to protect them as much as possible. But it seems to me that this action is more a natural reflex than one that stems from a true love for life itself. Is there not the real danger that we more and more and ever so slowly lose the notion of the meaning of our life?

I must admit that the question about the meaning of life is exceedingly difficult. What do we mean when we ask that question? A simple example may help to clarify the issue. Here I write down some words: *the silver moonlight radiated businessmen across the waters.*

The term "businessmen" makes no sense in the preceding string of words. It means something, of course, it says something, but it has no real meaning. Why is that? Because it is out of place there and does not fit in. It is situated as an indigestible lump amidst those other words. It does damage and prevents meaning more than it helps and supports. Somewhere else the word may fit perfectly, but here it just makes for nonsense. So when does a word make sense? It makes sense when it can seamlessly melt away in the context, when it fits in the totality. When does the life of a human make sense? It only makes sense when it has harmoniously inserted itself into the greater meaningful totality, when it is a part of an overall world concept.

Only when we have a much wider outlook on life will we be able to see the meaning of life and our place in it. Let me take an example. Suppose each human life represents a musical note, a note that sounds loud and then fades away. It could be a long note or short, a musical one or an atonal one, but all by itself it makes no sense. It only makes sense when we can be sure that, in the symphony of life, something is being expressed, that it is an integral part, a very tiny note in the immense gigantic symphony of the spheres that resounds continually through the expanse of the universe. Our note may be drowned in the totality of the orchestral performance, but its value remains. It is like our speech: our words also die after we have spoken them, but their meaning lives on. In that same sense people come and go, they are born and die, but in the end the divine intention, God's majestic plan for the world, will become visible.

Allow me to use another, more concrete example. Picture a businessman. Let me assume that it is his unmistaken desire to become rich in the shortest possible time. With that intent in mind he employs every means to reach that goal and pursues it single-mindedly. It is obvious that this man would see making money as the most important goal in his life, gathering in riches. Even though he sees that as the most important, even though that consumes him completely, it cannot constitute the meaning of his life. The real meaning is that he is part of a larger context. Through his enterprise he takes part in the overall culture and the total development of his country. Through his example, in his day-to-day dealings, by the way he interacts he has an impact, perhaps a good one, perhaps a bad one. Through his life the problems of his era are either brought more clearly into focus, are solved, or changed in other ways. In any case, his life amounts to something, is part of the totality, a facet of a larger structure. Long after he has retired to his country home, contentedly enjoying the fruits of his labor, some of his accomplishments still live on because in his ventures he has touched the lives of others, be it for good or ill. In the end he dies, and with it his influence. What is the meaning of his life? Certainly not what he himself saw as his priority.

When we look even deeper, take in the even larger picture, then we end up in front of the figure of Jesus Christ. Jesus tells us, not once but repeatedly, that the ultimate meaning of human life is the kingdom of God. It is possible that the light of God may enter into the human soul, the light that calls us and beckons us. To possess that light we often have to offer everything we have; it is the pearl of great value, for which we have to sacrifice all that we have. Of course we can ignore this call. Of course we can continue on the treadmill of sin and selfishness. But whatever we do, however we live, there always is something astir in our lives, there always are eternal powers at work, struggling for the welfare of our souls. There always is, in everybody's existence, something that pulls us. Jesus is always at work. Behind all these seemingly insignificant human actions, in all our life experiences, Jesus shows us something of immense importance. He makes us see that we can wrestle ourselves free from the grip of God, but also that we must humble ourselves before God so that the kingdom of God may fill our entire lives. Measured by that criterion everything makes sense, every human act contains something of value. In our struggle in the world Jesus himself paves the way toward the coming of that same Kingdom, a unique part of God's mighty and fabulous plan. He planned it all that way. He is the ruler there. He is the invisible guide in all this. When we see it this deeply, then we don't need to ask what the meaning of life is. Then it is completely clear. That's why Jesus' answers to the burning questions regarding life are so marvelously simple. He shows us the ultimate, eternal meaning of human life.

Is this the reason why we today are so unsure about the sense of life — that we have lost the vision of the Kingdom? Is this the reason why our lives so often major in insignificant and itty-bitty chitchat because we don't know the behind-the-scenes eternal happenings upon which all else in our lives depends? Is this also the reason why, in the crisscrossing of events in our little lives, we no longer can discern the one overarching continuum, the all-decisive connection with God and his Kingdom?

CHAPTER EIGHT

God's Plan: The Grand Chess Game

We have mentioned how, amidst all the human agitations, God is busy perfecting his own great and marvelous plan. Before we continue, we must have a closer look at what this implies.

I am referring to a question that sooner or later pops up in each one of us: How can a God who governs everything allow evil to exist in this world? The question is so framed: "If it is true that there is a mighty God who rules over all, how is it possible that there is so much injustice and so much misery?" We right away think of the invalids, the lonely, those who have lost all hope, and those who experience nothing but depression and trouble. We think about the wars, the torture and oppression, and we are disturbed to see how so often the course of events is the opposite of what we regard as just and reasonable. It seems that there is no justice when dealing with the plight of people and nations. On the contrary, those who struggle for righteousness in spite of all the odds are trampled on and even killed by brute force, and there is no hand from above offering help and a solution. The entire world scene often resembles nothing but chaos without rhyme or reason. How does all that correspond with faith in God's grand and beautiful plan?

Behind this dilemma another problem emerges, one even more difficult and unfathomable: it seems that almost always the evil is more powerful than the good, that God loses out in the fight against wickedness. If it is true that a holy and just God governs the happenings in the world, then it would make sense that the pages of history would record the victory of good over evil, that God is stronger than all opposing forces, or rather: he rules the world and nothing can happen without his will. Only he is supreme. So when we look realistically at the world at large, then what we see is exactly the opposite. God comes out as the loser while the evil seems strong and powerful. Pious people who have vested their full trust in God are treated like dirt, thrown into prison and killed. The fate of the world is decided by military force, and those who would expect that God himself would appear on the battlefields as their co-combatant are bitterly disappointed. Far from glossing over these matters, the Good News tells of Jesus Christ as the One sent by God, and shows how he, of an unsurpassed noble state, God in human form, was grabbed by cruel hands and crucified. Yes, the Lord of the world suffers defeat against the powers of evil.

When we are confronted with this sort of question and others similar to it, then we immediately sense that we are encountering one of the most confounding mysteries ever experienced by our human brain. I don't believe that we will ever find a satisfactory explanation for these problems. Here we are like small children, with growing anxiety observing what's going on in this world, and by any stretch of imagination not being able to understand why all this plays out as it does.

However, while taking all this in, there are a few points we should not overlook, to prevent us from going astray.

There are three observations I want to make. In the first place, while deliberating the great questions regarding us and our place in the world, our primary requirement is an attitude of reverence and humility. There is a Japanese proverb that says, "Only in humility can we enter into the core of nature's holiness." The same applies to history; the deepest secrets of history are revealed only to those who approach them in great humility. Just as we saw earlier, with every contemplation over the existence of this world, we always encounter the great mystery that surpasses all our thinking; that's why, when considering what has happened we can only bow our heads, admitting lack of insight. We ourselves are still on the battlefield of world history; we, as yet, cannot oversee the scene, we have no inkling how it all will end, we just don't recognize the demarcation lines, and also we are not objective observers. On the contrary: we are small, inconsequential people, who only here and there spot a tiny strip of light in the dark night of the world's mysteries.

In the second place we often run the danger of blaming God for what, in the final analysis, is completely our fault. When we really want to verbalize the strategy of our modern world, then the best we can do is to say that our technical ability and our scientific capability have far exceeded our moral powers. We have acquired powerful insights but we are morally too weak to use them. In spite of all our technical accomplishments we are a proud and stubborn people, not worthy to possess such powers. Our knowledge and our expertise are totally disproportionate to our moral capacity. The essence of the current period in the world's history can be formulated in this way: the tumultuous turmoil of the nations among themselves is proof positive that power, including technical know-how, is a curse in disguise when it does not serve "love." Perhaps that is the ultimate meaning of what we experience from day to day. Perhaps God is trying to teach us this by way of blood and tears. If that is the case, then under no circumstances may we attribute our suffering and misery to God, because what we are experiencing is nothing but the bitter fruit of what we have sown. If we were able to see through and perceive everything, then I am sure we would hear God's voice, which even in our days can be heard beyond all the clamor of the world's happenings, calling us to reflection.

In the third place we have to guard ourselves against attaching importance only to outward appearances. It is possible that a good and noble cause may suffer defeat when pitted against the less worthy. A villain with a gun can, after all, easily overwhelm an unarmed saint. But that does not mean that what we call defeats are in effect defeats. Napoleon, at the end of his life, experienced that there are losses in battle that in the long run appear to be glorious victories. His eyes were opened to see that Jesus, who, viewed superficially, had suffered a terrible defeat against the power of evil when he died on the cross, exactly by means of that cross established a Kingdom that is still viable after thousands of years, so that even now millions of people confess him as their lord and king.

Now that we are touching upon these more intricate matters it is perhaps the opportune time to try to obtain a deeper insight by using a simple comparison. It seems to me that many of the difficulties that face us can be explained when we view them through the imagery of a chess game.

Those who have played chess against a much more skillful player recognize the peculiar experience of being forced into playing in a certain way. Every move fits into the plan of the opponent. You move a pawn, you take his bishop, and for a moment you think you have won. Only later you discover that this was exactly what your opponent had in mind: every one of your moves fitted into this plan. He had already thought five or six moves ahead; he already had considered every possibility and not you but he was in charge of the entire game. After a while, when the game unfolds further, it becomes plain that you can only do what he wants you to do. Your strategy has been determined by him, and you can only do his bidding. Every one of your moves will only result in speeding up his victory.

Seen in that way, the entire world at large is one enormous game of chess with white playing black. We the people are the pawns, living pawns, while others are bishops or rooks. We all serve an authority larger than ourselves. We can side with the white, allying with the light; we can also form an alliance with black, the forces of evil. This game has been going on for centuries. White makes a move; black goes on the attack. At times black takes an important piece and penetrates white's defense, giving him visions of victory. But all black's moves, however clever, however seemingly devastating, fit in the greater, wiser plan of white. In the end it will be apparent how, what first looked like a victory for black, is nothing but one great triumph for white.

While I write these observations, I again see before my eyes one of the most perilous moments in the history of the world, the point in time when all the world's problems were uniquely focused. That was the moment when Jesus lived and worked in the world. I can picture how the powers of black, the evil powers, attacked him, grabbed him from all sides, and finally crucified him. If there ever was a moment when white looked weaker than black, that was the time. That was God's great defeat. God seemed smaller and weaker than the power of evil. It looked as if the world had been turned upside down, as if the Creator was defeated by his creature, as if the power of love, the root source of the universe, had to bow down before the power of hate. But, behold, also this move by black, this seeming victory by black, in the course of the ages turned out to be a mighty victory for God. That same cross, on which the king of light was killed, was from the beginning included in God's all-encompassing plan for the world. Through that cross the power of sin has been broken and the kingdom of God has come with might. It looked for a while that the cross signified the defeat of God, but seen from a higher perspective the cross is the exact point where God poured out everything he had for us humans, when his love was revealed to us.

It is impossible for anyone to exactly pinpoint where we are today. The current world situation is too much in a flux. We see an incoherent mix of opinions and tensions. Nobody can predict where it all will end, but we all realize that we are experiencing an enormous judgment over all our useless human thinking and probing. When we abide in the faith that God's plan is being revealed in all the world's happenings, then we can affirm only this single truth – that when once the mist disappears and we clearly see what has really happened, we will realize that all other kingdoms have broken up and disappeared, that the only Kingdom that comes is the kingdom of God's love that has appeared to us in the cross of Jesus.

CHAPTER NINE

Our Idols: Money

We now would like to further investigate something most humans regard as their goals in life, the aims they really want to pursue. It is therefore of the utmost importance to outline what we consider the most desired objective to strive for, the source and root of what we really want to accomplish. We know that every one of us has a single deeply rooted desire to be able to employ our own particular talents. Deep down we want to really develop what lives in us so that the various gifts we have will be expressed to the full. Every one of us longs for a situation where we can give ourselves freely, where what we are is fully revealed. To attain this is a great and moral ideal, because it is rooted in the all-important law of service, discussed earlier. Presupposed here is the concept that we live in a world that makes sense.

We could base our life on this perfect assumption, which we may call the original ideal situation, but we know this cannot be done. There are other factors besides this deep longing that dominate our collective lives. There are other tendencies, stemming from the original source, and they push life in a totally wrong direction. They are the three idols that we will discuss now. First we will examine the great and almost irresistible desire for money, the factor that motivates and drives very many human lives and is the life motive in many of us.

When we discuss here the craving for money, we mean this in

the larger and deeper sense. We don't point to the few dollars we need to buy some chocolates. There's more to it than that. We all have, whether young or old, a continuous urge to become rich. If we were to approach a group of young people with the question of what they really want, most of them will probably say they want to be rich. To be rich sounds so romantic, especially for those who have absolutely no idea what it means. Money is the magic wand that unlocks the doors to elegant hotels, picturesque palaces, and glorious gardens. There's something quite enchanting about money, something that unlocks passionate pictures. If we want to fully understand its hypnotic power, we need look no further than the ubiquitous casinos where we can see how money can inflame people, make eyes sparkle, and totally possess them. Then we see how money is like a god, completely absorbing them.

When we ask why, several factors come to mind. In the first place the remarkable aspect of money is that in itself it is nothing, but it contains the promise to be everything. Money now is no more than a piece of paper or an entry in a ledger, but it allows me to buy everything I want. Money is pure possibility, pure potentiality. That is the real romance of the money-concept, something that at the same time gives it an awesome allure. Whatever we buy with it loses its luster after a while and fails to satisfy us, but this does not affect money as such because as yet it is nothing. That's why money is such a blurred, undefined image so capable of bewitching the true money seeker. But that too is the reason why it can exercise such divine power over the soul. All other matters disappoint because the idea of an object is always more beautiful than the object itself. Only money remains the throne of a god carrying many treasures in his hands and always ready with its magic words to unlock all the doors to beauty and splendor.

In the second place, money has the power to bedevil the human soul because it indemnifies a person and is compensation for sin. We notice this especially in connection with the secret longing alive in all people when they have the opportunity to utilize all their gifts and hidden potential. That is particularly the case when where we work we are able to employ all our talents, which then often results in doing better, rising above ourselves so to say, inspired by love for what we are doing. That means that love is the great treasure: love enables us to unlock the deepest and noblest tendencies in our hearts. However, that same discovery of our innate talents has a tendency to move us in a wrong direction, away from others towards "how will it benefit me!" At play are multiple factors, all pushing us to change course for our own benefit. Thoughts such as "I don't care how I make money, as long as I benefit from it" enter people's minds. Actually the full employment of our abilities can be at odds with life itself. It is as if we are trying to evade the tensions that are always part of life, as if, in a wave of radical pessimism, we deny life's reality. Our true aim in life is to become something, to be somebody. The wrong way to go about this is to have something, to be able to boast about our possessions. In reality this reveals, deeply hidden in us, an enmity against society, and, basically, against authority at large, against life in general. This sort of attitude says that helping others is a waste of effort. Everything is doomed to fail. I would rather have hard cash. Such behavior acts as compensation for having forfeited the true meaning of one's life by refusing to willingly and gladly support others.

There's yet more to it than that. Money also functions in a way that is even more magical. Having money means that a person's personality changes. Money is not merely something you possess: it also changes your makeup, changes who you are. It increases the value of your personality, it causes people to listen to you with greater interest, causes you to think more highly of yourself. You can be the smartest person, but when you land into a big city with no funds at all, and roam through the snow-covered streets and there's not a single place to go for a warm meal, then it's no wonder you feel down and out. On the other hand, you could be a nonentity in understanding and character, but when you are welcomed everywhere with open arms and people cater to you because you are rich, then sooner or later you start to imagine that you really are somebody. That's what money does to people. It causes them to see themselves differently and it lends to their personality a certain flair. That flair makes them stand out, causes other people to treat them differently, to become friendlier, to honor them and try hard to please them. Especially for those who possess little else, money is everything. Take away that dollar sign and they revert back to the emptiness of nothing. Were they to be robbed of their wealth, they'd be robbed simultaneously of their self-worth, their totality, life itself. The opposite is true as well. Those who really signify something, who amount to something in the world, can treat money with a degree of indifference. They can easily travel tourist class on the airplane, and will without blushing admit that they are short of cash. They smilingly confess that money means little to them because they know their value to society. They can afford the luxury of poverty because, in spite of a lack of funds, they still are valuable persons.

And still there is more to it. Money offers still more. Money allows in many ways the possibility to increase life's opportunities. That really is the most beautiful function of money. It opens up the expansion of universities and helps to spread literature. It offers opportunities to develop the spirit and sharpen the brain. In general it paves the way to far more employment opportunities where responsible people can develop their full potential. That's why there are so many low-income parents who dream about money, who wrestle with money to enable their children to have better economic prospects.

Having taken a closer look at the influence of money, then, we are impressed with its power. It has an aura of romance; it's like a god because it accomplishes divine miracles. When life proves disappointing, when our soul is full of turmoil, struggling with many unsolved tensions, then money comes to the rescue and makes us feel comfortable. There are many who live unsatisfactory and useless lives, but for them money is the medicine that can cure the inner dissatisfaction. When life frightens us because we ourselves are often such unhappy misfits, money gives compensation, reinforces our ego, lifts us up out of the doldrums, and causes us to imagine that we amount to something. That's why it enhances our self-worth, at least our idea of self-worth. In the last place it offers us the opportunity for more and better self-enhancement and, in this way, enables us to more closely approach our potential. All this is money at work, and it accomplishes this by not being anything in itself. It is pure opportunity. It is nothing, yet it can mean everything. It is a substance that lifts our entire life to a different level. Isn't that what a god does? Isn't that divine power?

And yet all three different conditions contain an illusion; all give a terrible misdirection. Agreed, money offers comfort, but surely not true comfort. Yes, it opens the door to possessions, but it does nothing for what really counts in life. Money does not bring love, health, a long and blessed life, nor does it guarantee insight or inner peace and happiness. It is a ticket to everything on the market but cannot buy the only item that makes life pleasant. Money does give a degree of comfort, but it is a false one, it is merely a substitute.

Money does add something to one's personality: it gives a person a notion of creditability. It causes a person to walk with greater confidence. It enhances the ego. But all this extra bravura is a sham. "The emperor has no clothes," as the saying goes. Money means nothing in terms of eternity. A nonentity with a nice suit is still a nonentity. In essence money is an illusion, and that is the reason why money prevents a person from really understanding the true self.

Agreed, money allows persons to more easily develop their talents and their influence, but that does not guarantee redemption. It does not generate new insights into one's soul, does not produce new character traits. It leaves persons essentially what they are. Money is not a moral force; it does not sanctify a person. It offers the possibility to develop mental and aesthetical gifts, but it does not create them. It cannot stimulate a refined sense or a deeper inner life. It cannot work a "metanoia," a rebirth.

Let's face it: money is a god. In the human soul the money-concept is intertwined with romantic feelings; it fills our mood with secret longings. But when we bare the true image of this god, we see that it is, indeed, an idol, and an idol is, in essence, a lie.

All this comes really into focus when we watch Jesus' approach to money. When we compare the two, Jesus and money, then we cannot help smiling. I don't mean to say that Jesus did not recognize the usefulness of money, that he did not use it. But when he saw the role money plays in many a human heart, that of a miracle-working god, then he totally objected to it. He forcefully required of people to give away everything they possessed. In no uncertain terms he posed the choice for people: God or Mammon. Money has all the functions of an idol, and that's why it derives its strength from the deep and ineradicable human need for God. After all, our soul thirsts for God. But if money fosters that urge and seemingly satisfies that craving, then it is one colossal lie.

That's why, by radically turning all values upside down, Jesus could say with that holy emphasis which is the secret to his entire being, "What does it benefit people when they would gain the entire world, all the money in the world, yet forfeit their souls?" In matters eternal what really matters is not what we possess but who we are. "Blessed are the poor in spirit." They find grace with the real God, who is both much stronger than money and also much more merciful because he is the eternal and holy power.

CHAPTER TEN

Our Idols: Honor

"A good name is better than good oil," said one of the wisest men ever, thousands of years ago. Indeed, a good name is a treasure worth a fortune, because it has great value.

It's not difficult to show why this is the case, and quite simple when we take as point of departure the ultimate human ideal, the almost impossible goal of arriving at a harmonious development of our innermost being. After all, if we want to discover this sublime state, with every step in that direction we need the appreciation and trust of our fellow humans. These finest of personality traits can only come to fruition in an atmosphere of fidelity and love. Only when these are present will the buds of the precious flower that is the human soul open up. That is something everybody feels intuitively.

Both honor and reputation are indispensable for our entire lives. Without them we angrily languish while vengefully blaming people for misunderstanding us.

All that is self-evident, so much so that we right away condemn others when they deal too harshly with the delicate fabric of people's good reputation. There are at times also those who make wild accusations without any basis whatsoever, thereby deeply hurting people's feelings and causing all sorts of commotion, which only earns them the label of fools and good-for-nothings. When this backfires on them, such people often blame the world at large because they fail to recognize that those who harm someone's good name are well on the way to trampling on their own happiness. Just as our body needs air to breathe, so our soul needs trust, appreciation, and honor in order to be able to express itself. That is one of the basic laws of human wisdom.

That's also the reason why, in a last-ditch effort to rescue a person from proceeding on the road to self-destruction, we try to appeal to his sense of honor. If a person cannot stop sinning, because of his alcohol addiction or whatever, we may resort to reminding him of the pain caused to his mother or father, and, if even that falls on deaf ears, to his feelings of self-worth. We may say something like, "Come on, act like a man, make people look up to you!" When this final effort also fails, when his final reply is "I don't care what others think," then he is pretty well lost. Then the last attempts to rescue his soul have come to nothing.

And still, however strange this may sound, this honoring, this appreciation, can be an idol. What should be a means becomes a goal. For instance, rather than trying to make ourselves better people, we do something for the sake of pure self-promotion. This is also the case when we pursue a certain plan that only we see as desirable, even necessary, so we stop listening to others. When that happens, we undergo an eclipse of the soul. Then the truth is obscured by the lie, pushing it further and further away.

Let me use a simple example. I am the speaker at a gathering and in an eloquent presentation I am trying to plead for a good cause. I use all sorts of arguments; I use all the tricks of the trade, so to say, to convince the audience and move them to action. All goes well. As long as I have the floor, things go smoothly. I am there to promote a cause. It's the cause that is important. What really counts is that with all I have at my disposal I advance a worthy goal that deserves the best of my efforts. Of course when I speak I am not indifferent as to whether people listen to me or not. And, yes, I should really care, because I want to convince people and move them to action. I fight for their attention; I do all I can to gain trust, not for my own sake, but for the cause I serve. The cause is what matters. I finish with a flourish and sit down, followed by a thunderous applause. People congratulate me on my skillful presentation. Then a thought pops up in my mind, "I did a pretty good job there," and there the trouble starts. Right away I am more important than the cause. I glorify in hearing that people admired my words, not so much that the cause I promoted was good, but that I did such a good job. Suddenly it's me that is on top. No longer do I serve the cause; no, the cause serves me, gives me the glory. When later, in that same room, another person comes up and with even greater eloquence defends that same cause so that people respond even more enthusiastically, I feel a bit irritated. Of course it's good for the cause, but I feel somewhat slighted. That is the moment when a change takes place in my soul and the course of my life takes a wrong turn. What served as a means has now become a goal. At first I was a servant, using my talents in promoting a good cause; now the soul dominates, trying to win over people by means of a good cause. There's where the difference lies.

We, as people, are not all the same in matters such as this. It all depends on our own inner security, on the way we see ourselves.

There are strong personalities among us, people who almost from birth have a natural confidence that what they say or do is beyond dispute. They are sure of themselves; their opinions are right, their conclusions correct. Because they are so self-assured it is easy for them to ignore other people's insights. They don't easily give in when encountering opposition. That does not mean they do not pursue "honor." Deep in their hearts they crave recognition but they are sure enough of themselves not to be discouraged when for the moment this seems to slip away. Their self-assurance does not desert them. Yet they too look for the moment of applause: they are far more dependent on human approval than they themselves realize.

There are also those who, by nature, are very insecure. They never are completely sure of themselves and always scared that they have done or said something wrong. They are always hesitant when it concerns doing something because in their minds they are so confused. It is natural that such weak characters look much more for encouragement in others. They constantly are on the lookout for reaction to their words and actions. In their inner insecurity they aim for support, crave approval and admiration. In all cases others set the tone for what they are. They are so at odds with themselves that their eyes always are on those around them for approval.

Between these two extremes there is a multitude of nuances. There are those who, with a loud mouth, make little sense; others seem confident but inside are consumed by fear and insecurity. Among all these there are bizarre variations and eccentric diversities. But what all these people have in common is that what is supposed to be the means, and as such quite valuable, becomes of primary importance.

This small, or rather seemingly small, reorientation causes a drastic reversal in the human psyche. This too can be easily illustrated. There is no better way to do this than by contrasting this deviation to the ideal situation where the cause is all-important. We all possess gifts, the gift of music or painting, the gift of scholarship, of business or commerce, or of lovingly caring for others. We want to use these gifts to be of service to the community at large. It's not about us but about the cause, about what we can give. The message comes first, and because that is the case we rise above other people. It's all about serving others, and we do this for the sake of love, but we don't do this slavishly. The message is the redeeming factor, not gaining favor with people. When we want to move people to listen to us, this is only for their sake and not for self-promotion. We are merely the messengers, under the message and above the people: we are like a serving ruler — above everybody else but at the same time servant of all.

On the other hand, we become a slave when, due to a change inside us, our primary goal is being appreciated and gathering kudos. When that is the case, instead of serving a cause, the cause serves us, as we drink in the compliments that feed our egos. The result is that we depend on others, become their slave, and their applause and their loyalty becomes a necessity. We no longer are prophets but beggars for human acceptance, and in the process we sink deeper than we ever could imagine. That is the radical spiritual change that makes us totally different people. Something has completely reversed our attitude. That's why, from there on, we no longer see others in an unbiased light, but perceive them either as those who applaud us or as those who disapprove. We feel affronted by those who disapprove of us. We no longer see the cause, but see the people because we have become prejudiced. It's no longer the cause that matters. Interjected between us and our eloquence and our most beautiful testimony always pops up that little idol "Me." We can never completely free ourselves from that condition.

In his book *Führer Europas* the historian Emil Ludwig tells us a story about the end of the Great War (1914-18). He relates how on November 9, 1918, Winston Churchill and Lloyd George deliberated the next step. They discussed whether or not the best course would be to dispatch a few boatloads of food to Germany where blockades had caused widespread famine. This would provide a real basis for reconciliation between Great Britain and Germany founded on moral grounds. At that critical moment they did not dare to take that step, afraid as they were that their supporters, still burning with hatred against Germany, would not approve this. When in December of that same year Lloyd George spoke everywhere in connection with the upcoming election, his speeches were full of hate against the vanquished enemy: he pleased the voting public where it wanted to be flattered. In that he was so successful that more than 80 percent voted for him. "But," writes Ludwig, "it remains true, that Lloyd George, who during the war acted with energy and wisely conducted himself in peace, within two months succumbed to the instincts of crowd pleaser by flattering the masses rather than educating them." At that solemn moment, when the future of building a new Europe was at stake, he was unable to rise above himself, too afraid of losing the public's approval so precious to him. If persons want to be served by a cause, the inevitable result is that they become slaves of their fellow citizens. In the deciding moments of world history this has again and again proved to be the most horrible mistake.

All this comes directly into focus when we for a moment look deeper into the life of Jesus. He was the most naïve of all, naïve in the sense that he always surrendered himself to his task, his message, and was subject to his cause and stood above the people. "I don't seek honor!" (John 8:50). Never do we spot his eyes surveying the crowd for a word of praise or applause. Never do we detect in one of his words the tiny idol that at once deprives humans of their goodness. Jesus always stands below his message when he says, "I honor the Father!" Come to think of it, it is only when we as strongly as possible try to fathom what Jesus really wants us to do, that we realize how far off the mark we are. The most saintly among us, those able to convey the tidings of Good News and live lives of constant testimony, still are no more than dethroned rulers, compared to him.

There always is the little idol called "honor" that soils our soul. Never can we do without this tiny god called "honor" that keeps us from fully serving the cause.

CHAPTER ELEVEN

Our Idols: The Pursuit of Pleasure

Amidst the multitude of influxes that agitate within us we have, especially now, the time we live in, scores of complicated and miraculous diversions, all fueled by our relentless pursuit of pleasure. The ancient Romans clamored for two of life's overriding distractions: bread and games. Both of these represented the sum total of all the favorite pastimes for which their hearts yearned. Quite similar to that life, the majority of people today are moved by identical forces.

When we analyze the pursuit of pleasure, we right away sense that this involves a host of peculiar factors. By itself pleasure is a very strange phenomenon. Basically it is something that automatically accompanies every single act of a successfully completed project. Here is a simple example. I am working at a mathematical problem. For quite some time the problem has kept me thinking without coming to a solution. Then, out of the blue, I discover how to solve it. I do some further calculations and find out that this is indeed the way to go. Then my eyes light up, something pleasurable wells up in my mind, and triumphantly I proceed to the definite solution. Pleasure is a companion of a job well done.

If a smartly moving train locomotive had a consciousness, it would thoroughly enjoy speeding over the smooth rails across the countryside. A craftsman carefully completing some kitchen cabinets, or a scientist deeply deliberating some problems, or a merchant by making amends here and there and so managing to complete a lucrative deal, in short, whoever does something and does it enthusiastically for the good of society will always experience great pleasure upon completion. Intense joy is a byproduct of a job that is completed with heart and soul.

Actually upon second thought, all this makes perfect sense. The grand goal of everyone's life, our overriding objective, is, after all, the quiet harmonious unfolding of our talents and potential. That always is a joyful experience: the one is not possible without the other.

I don't have to emphasize that this blissful feeling is also felt when we do workouts, one reason why we also have organized sports. On the other hand to relax after hours of toil, to sit down and quietly read the newspaper or listen to music can also generate similar sensations of pleasure. For all these reasons joy occupies an important place in our lives and fills a great part there, be it in many little ways. Many of our life experiences are embroidered with an emblem of joy, which we hardly notice because it is like a faint glimmer, sometimes only visible when we ourselves are in the dark. That's why sometimes, perhaps far later or when far away, when we look back to earlier times they can appear to us as a clear, sun-drenched landscape. The fact is that there is much more joy in our lives than we usually suspect.

However, in the life of untold many people a remarkable separation has taken place between labor and entertainment. Work is increasingly seen as something necessary but onerous, a continual burden, while the seeking of pleasure has become as an oasis in the desert of labor. Life has become a shift into two areas, into two very carefully separated parts, that of duty and pleasure, work and recreation. Only the latter is seen as joyful, as pleasurable. The former is increasingly regarded as devoid of pleasure, as shorn of joy, as robbed of the glow of fulfillment. I don't want to elaborate how this shift came about, how part of our lives has soured on us. No doubt there are many social and special cultural factors that play a role in this transition. Of course, the technicization of much of what we produce is a major factor in this process. But whatever is the case, the facts are clear: in our days, labor and pleasure are seen as two completely separate fields, as two totally opposite entities.

Because of this peculiar split, entertainment too has assumed a very different character. It has had to be freed, as much as possible, from all traces of work. All sorts of pleasures that require a measure of exertion, such as attending a good concert or reading an interesting book, are being degraded as too labor intensive. Pleasure is relegated to doing nothing, to getting intoxicated, to behaving foolishly, to mindlessly watching television while sport by and large has become a passive affair. In this way in general recreation has become a way of life, an idol for which we live. The slice of life devoted to pure entertainment has become the only part that is seen as worthwhile, the remainder as necessary evil. All this has further resulted in a pursuit of pleasure that, especially in large urban centers, has started to assume frightening proportions.

I am not going to elaborate in what forms these amusements have developed because such a detailed description would require too much explanation. My main thesis is to affirm the absolute schism between work and enjoyment that has taken place in the consciousness of so many people.

However, I will in a few words point to a remarkable phenomenon that is directly related to these matters. In the first place I will mention that the separation between work and enjoyment has severely impoverished both. Because work is viewed as something without mental merit, this has resulted in expecting from amusement such a high reward that it has become impossible to satisfy this expectation. That brief instant of enjoyment now must so serve in capturing the essence of fun so that it also can compensate for the lack of pleasure in the workplace. Of course that is a requirement that no form of entertainment in the long run can fulfill. However much our technical know-how is increasingly capable of refining and intensifying our entertainment, it is simply not possible to satisfy our urge for increasingly stronger stimulations. No wonder that dissatisfaction with life is becoming more pronounced.

Part of this can be traced to the difficulty for pleasure to multiply itself. Simple accounting cannot be applied to pleasure. With other items the usual rule is simple: $1 + 1 = 2$. One apple + another apple = two apples. But this does not apply to enjoyment. The sensation of eating a piece of cake and then eating another piece does not give double satisfaction. The first few bites will tickle our taste buds, but after those we certainly will not increase our enjoyment. On the contrary. This applies to every stimulant. The elation that is felt with the first airplane trip, the first time moving into a new dwelling, is never reached in successive similar experiences. Everything reverts back to normal. In the world of pleasurable matters 1 + 1 never = two, but always less than two. That also applies to the poverty of riches. A rich person may be able to spend twice as much for a trip as a common worker, who has to scrimp to afford a less classy excursion, but double the outlay does not mean double the enjoyment. The wealthy may spend ten or twenty times as much to furnish their mansion as a young couple just starting out, but that does not entail that they will have the same proportion of happiness. In the world of enjoyable experiences the laws of multiplication simply do not apply. Doubling the expenses means at best a 50 percent increase in enjoyment. A luxurious tour, eating in first-class restaurants, sleeping in five-star hotels, may not equal that simple bike ride with a homemade lunch and a bottle of juice tucked away in the bicycle bag. There simply are no comparisons. The main point is that doubling the expenses and doubling the extent of opportunities never means the simple multiplication of doubling the enjoyment. There, 1 + 1 never = 2.

When we closely study these matters in their context, we notice that we all divide life into two parts: work and enjoyment. If we must really derive our happiness and joie de vivre from this tiny amount of amusement, then no wonder that we find ourselves at a dead end. Why? Because in order to get a greater kick out of life we constantly need ever-stronger doses of amusement. Since this is impossible we increasingly become more dissatisfied. Life simply cannot provide us with what we need. Amusement as a little god in isolation cannot possibly satisfy our needs for recreation. That's the reason why many are thoroughly fed up with life, a situation that has become an epidemic which is making life intolerable for many: suicide is now one of the leading causes of death.

Escaping this mix-up is only possible when our daily work and the drive to enjoy ourselves blend more and more, and complement each other. Only by making life more unified, when joy exists in self-development, when we offer ourselves as living sacrifices, only this sort of surrender offers the strongest guarantee against dissatisfaction. In the final analysis it always reverts back to the basic ideal condition: the only real ground for joy in our lives is to surrender ourselves with all that is within us and thus with all our gifts and powers serve that great and divine calling: to love God and his creation above all and our neighbors as ourselves. Only by doing this do we find our joy.

That is not something we embrace right away. We only really begin to see this when we come closer to Jesus. Jesus' life is one radiant example of service and surrender, expressed in his words: "My life is to do the will of my heavenly Father." For him this comes naturally. Of course, there are no idols in his life. The salt in his life never becomes tasteless, never loses its power. His entire life is one of complete gratitude, giving thanks when he walks along the roads, giving thanks while doing his daily work, giving thanks when he lies down to rest. His life flows like a brook, clear as crystal. That's why in him all of life's questions find their solution.

For those who have never before or have ceased to take delight in the act of service, who no longer practice self-surrender, or doing the will of the heavenly Father, they now need three idols. These people need money to upgrade life to a higher level. They need the intoxicating stimulant of honor to artificially elevate their ego, and they need enjoyment to quench their thirst for amusement. These three, viewed in this way by themselves and contrasted to the ideal "service" situation, really are idols: they are the unholy trinity of sin. They entice and seduce, they cajole and lure, and yet these three are no more than mere illusions. All three lack substance; they contain nothing, have no lasting value, are far too insubstantial to ever satisfy the hunger in the human heart.

All three are like whirlpools sucking in life. They swallow us up and suffocate us. No human being can wrestle free and escape their attraction, not you, not me. There is only One. Meditating on life's questions only leads to one conclusion, only makes us perhaps grudgingly acknowledge that there ever has been only one human being who knew what life was all about, who alone lived life in true fashion, who alone placed himself outside those three illusions, who did not bow the knee for the trinity of sin. That was Jesus. That's why all of life's questions are concentrated in him: "Lord, teach us how to live!"

Only he gives the solution. We who struggle can only expect to live when we take as point of departure the faith that God's world makes sense, that we live in a world created by the eternal Father. When we rely on that tender belief that he also has given us life, talents, and powers, and that he has placed us where we ought to be, when we do nothing there but shine our little light and quietly serve, and when we really believe that the Father is all and in all, then we really don't need the unholy trinity. Then we live life as a child. Then we live the only true ideal way of life, the only way worth living, by accomplishing the task the Father gave us.

When we really are up to that kind of life, yes, going against the stream, when we really believe so strongly in him, when we really believe that everything in life has its place and everybody a task, a way of life destined and assigned by the Lord, then we have learned what life is all about. To live is to serve in the full confidence that we are here in a world that makes sense, believing that an all-wise Father is our guide.

CHAPTER TWELVE

Sin

Let's face it: sin is not an attractive word, but nevertheless we just can't ignore the issue. We have just dealt with the three idols that have infiltrated and seduced us, as it were, and we also have seen how little we are capable of resisting these forces. Our lives are filled with defects, errors, misunderstandings, faults, and shortcomings. Yet to acknowledge that is not the same as to speak of "sin." The concept of sin contains elements that go far deeper and have far more serious implications.

In order to understand this correctly it is desirable for a moment to probe how we can explain the imperfections and the weaknesses we have detected in our lives.

In the first place it seems likely that many of these shortcomings can be traced to our sheer stupidity and ignorance. We often are like a blind child, living and acting without really knowing what we do. We allow ourselves to be swept along by our passions and influenced by our senses and only rarely do we question why. There's so much insensitive stupidity in our lives. When we today consider the senseless wars, especially against creation, combined with the artificially generated hatred against other people and religions, now a worldwide phenomenon, then we realize how not only we as individuals but the entire world is blind to the real state of the planet. Gone is all rational thinking. Gone is all sensible reflection. There only is greed, there only is artificiality and mind-intoxication. We cannot fully blame the military establishment when, in the heat of battle, a soldier aims his weapon at defenseless citizens: he then doesn't act as a conscious, rational being, possessed as he is by dark demons. And the same is true for so much of what we do because many of our actions are influenced by our energy-drunkenness, sprouting out of the sinister instincts that possess us, all fueled by motives that are stronger than we. Buddhism teaches us that the deepest root of all evil is ignorance. It is that delusion that has captivated us.

In the second place it seems that a large part of what we lack can be blamed on the society in which we are born, can be placed at the feet of our parents and teachers, and can be traced to the books we have read and to the many others who have made us what we are. There was a time when the favorite expression was that we are a product of circumstances. We interpreted "circumstances" to mean the total of all influences that have formed us from our infancy till now. The prevailing notion was that "circumstances" formed our character, steered life in a certain direction and gave it structure. In later life we could detect the way we conducted ourselves by ticking off all the factors that contributed to our character formation.

In the third place we would be inclined to blame a large portion of our character flaws on the peculiarly dualistic composition of our being. We have brains, we can utilize our spiritual and rational powers, but at the same time we are physically weak creatures. We can glory in being capable of lofty sentiments, can utter noble thoughts, but sooner or later we tumble back into cruel reality. Simple physical factors – fatigue, hunger, pain, sensuality – all can create havoc in our innermost being, never before thought imaginable.

When we focus on these three considerations, we can, in our mind, fully acknowledge our defects and faults and still not even come close to the concept of "sin." We can even admit that we suffer from a complex set of contradictions and are chock-full of character deviations, and yet, with tooth and nail we resist the concept of "sin." We can readily confess that we are prone to errors. We can even say that we are, in many ways, objects of pity, poor misfits who time and again shut the door to our happiness – but being sinful, being sinners? No, that we are not. Where does it come from that we so abhor the word *sin*? Or to take a different tack, what is included in the word *sin* that does not form part of the word *shortcoming*?

The word *sin* is so significant because it includes two particular concepts. In the first place the word *sin* always has the connotation of a measure of intent and signifies surrender to reality. If I acknowledge my sin, then I admit that my flaws and defects are my responsibility and belong on my own balance sheet. The Good News completely allows for acceptance of all the excuses we have listed before. When Jesus was being crucified by sinful human hands, he prayed for his enemies because, so he said, "they don't know what they are doing." Indeed, our human frailties are to a large degree a product of our ignorance, and that same ignorance can, to some extent, serve as excuse. But there always remains that other element, our distorted will. Those who lived in Jerusalem could have given numerous reasons to justify why they had not followed Jesus. They could have reasoned that they had been misled by their teachers, or had been blinded by nationalistic fervor. But when Jesus at a certain moment characterizes their true attitude, then he points to their real motive: "You refused to follow me!" Behind all our human deviations, behind all our faults, lies a measure of unwillingness, of obstinacy. We love the darkness and take delight in wandering there. When we come to our senses, when we are made aware of our shortcomings, then we are inclined to become angry and stick to our guns. The essential element in the concept of sin is that I own up to my defects and that I confess that the sinful will within me wants me to prolong my shortcomings.

In the second place the concept of sin includes the factor that sin has a close connection to God. Sin always has a God-factor. The real reason for denying sin is our constant effort to wrestle free from God and to resist his will. Just as for a child the concept of evil is of necessity connected to their relationship to their parents, by going against what they desire, in the same way the word *sin* contains an inexpressible element that whatever we do has a direct relation to God who has determined the way we should go. As long as I talk about our defects, our errors, I can safely remain on a horizontal plane, and observe only the earthly connection, but as soon as I use the word *sin* I enter into the vertical sphere and observe the tie that binds our life to the eternal. I then admit that I sin against God, and I place myself as a rebel over against him and obstruct the order he has destined for my life.

The Bible speaks a lot about God. One of the themes that constantly come to the fore is that he is the Holy God. It is not easy to gauge the meaning of the word *holy* to its fullest extent, but one of the thoughts included therein is illustrated as follows: "God, your eyes are too pure to look on evil; you cannot tolerate wrongdoing" (Habakkuk 1:13). God, the almighty, turns his eyes away from all those vile human doings. He pushes away all that seeking after money and honor that occupies our life. One of the Psalms says: "Nobody alive is justified before your face." When the concept of God's majesty and holiness really takes hold of us, when we finally start to realize who he is who penetrates our lives into the furthest crevices, only then we begin to realize what the word *sin* really contains. Admit it: I am a slave to the three idols: money, honor, pleasure. I am chained to the vile powers that imprison me. If all looks quite well judging by appearances, the heart of the matter is a different story. The cruel truth is that I have become alienated from my Father in the heavens; I have sneaked away from his community and lived a life that, in every aspect, is against his will. Now I stand before him as a sinner, as one who has refused to do his will.

Only when we have come to that confession, do we enter into the sphere of the Good News. Only then the Good News starts to mean something for us. Then Jesus sees us and he enters into our life. If I want to pronounce the word *sin*, then God responds by saying redemption. Only when I acknowledge the first can the second be fulfilled in me.

CHAPTER THIRTEEN

The Cry for Deliverance

The original vision of human calling was service in its fullest scope and doing this gladly with all we possess. That was truly evident when God specified these conditions to the first human pair, at their creation, entrusting them with the care for his cosmos. This was then and still is now our great cultural mandate. The faint notions of this original assignment are still visible to us, actually becoming more evident now that creation is in such a state of imbalance.

When we look into this somewhat more closely, it is striking that it reminds us of the great and noble powers given to us at the time of creation. They were given to us with the express purpose to develop them, to deploy them, and so use them to serve God. It is true that we have many diverse abilities and talents, both physical and spiritual, but at the top of these are the three aforementioned: knowledge, peace with the Highest, and holiness. Those three are the traits that give us humans our unique stamp, lending us a character that distinguishes us from every other creature, making us rational, spiritual, and moral beings. These three profound traits are so important that they deserve further elaboration. This will help us greatly when we deal with some other, related issues.

Concerning that special knowledge, it has to be seen in its proper perspective. There are several sorts of knowledge, not every form of which possesses the same value. In the first place there is factual knowledge, which concerns things – just that. Take a chestnut tree.

I know what it looks like and can distinguish it from other trees. I know my house, my city, my friend; I know gold, silver, wood, iron, etc. I am acquainted with other persons, I am familiar with lots of tidbits; that is to say I've heard of them, which means my knowledge is quite superficial. It may come in handy someday to know all that but it doesn't really amount to much.

A second form of knowledge is that I know where something comes from. When the lamp in my room suddenly goes out, it is important to know the reason. I then not only know the fact but also learn the cause of that happening and so, if I can change the way it happened, I myself can bring about a change in the situation. An even higher form of knowledge is that I also know where matters end up, what their destination is. I know what a chestnut tree looks like, but I also know what we can do with its fruit, its trunk, and its roots. In that case I can utilize the object of my knowledge in practical ways, and can even make my knowledge profitable, as I have a good overview of the entire matter. All these forms of knowledge have a certain value in our day-to-day affairs. Yet none of these examples of knowledge counts for anything at all when earlier we mentioned that knowledge is one of the highest goals in human life, because there is a much higher form of knowledge.

We can also know the world as the revelation of the Divine Being, as the expression of his essence. Every being, small or great, contains a divine design, and every being is at the same time maintained by God's power and wisdom. That means that God is at the center of all that exists, the basis on which everything rests, the anchor that holds it all in place. As soon as we know matters in their relationship to him, as his revelation, only then have we gauged their real character and finally reached the core of the matter. All other knowledge remains on the surface, is still on the periphery. Only when we draw the line to the center can we measure its totality. That's why the highest form of knowledge is the one that sees all things reflecting divine splendor, having a godly halo. It is precisely this form of knowledge that we almost totally lack. We are amazingly capable of determining the how and the why and for what purpose we use things, but the question of what their essence is, of how they fit into the totality of things, that is a question we cannot even pose, let alone solve. That's the reason we must openly confess that the real knowledge, the knowledge of God, and the knowledge of the world in God, is something we totally lack.

We must come to that same dreadful conclusion when we contemplate the matter of peace. We must see peace as the state in which we live in a harmonious relationship with the Divine, so that there is a creation-loving, shalom-like interdependence between us and our God. This is indeed a mutual affair.

In the first place we can state that we must, with all our faculties, direct our life in God's service. Just as a flower always tends to turn to the light, just as the compass needle always points to the North, driven by invisible magnetism, so too our compass needle must always point to the eternal Origin. And that too makes sense. Water, for instance, may evaporate and, as such, rise up high above the earth, but once there, it condenses again, and, as rain, returns back to the earth, because it belongs to the earth. In that same way it makes sense that we too refer back to God, as through his Spirit, our heart and soul are aimed his way.

We also can reverse the issue. God also desires peace, harmony, and solitude. And here we must make a sad admission: we, in our lives, experience with ever-increasing certainty that our relationship with the Most High has completely been severed. Our very own "soul" compass no longer points to God, but is aimed with increasingly pronounced clarity to ourselves as the goal of our lives. We always are engaged, whether we realize it or not, in serving ourselves and seeking our well-being, and the forces aimed at seeking God are very weak and seldom come into play. In addition we often have the feeling that God, as it were, opposes us, that God is justified to reject us, to punish and to threaten us. We feel banned from God's presence, rejected by him, as persons who everywhere face punishment, as persons who sooner or later face the death penalty. Our relationship with God is not harmonious; justice is indeed a requirement, is indeed needed to make life livable, but, as we see each day more clearly, a just society is far from reality. The evidence is irrefutable that people everywhere in the world suffer these injustices, plainly evident in their frightful conditions and their painful experiences.

When we finally ask the question of where we stand in relation to our state of holiness, then we must come to the same sad conclusion. It may be true that in our mind we always retain something of the majesty of goodness, but that does not exclude the fact that our lives are often hiding places of enormous amounts of sin. Also it is striking how egoistic we often are, evident in the harshness we display when confronting others. All people are different: one may be a perfect liar, another quite loose with morality, and a third one filled with bitterness towards his fellows. When we dig a bit deeper into what goes on around us, and especially when we have learned to separate appearance from reality, the results often are very discouraging. Calling us holy appears to be quite an exaggeration. In our hearts we humans carry a goodly number of passions, and we are loath to reveal these most intimate thoughts to others, because we are well aware that they are not at all what they should be.

We are well aware that we are far, far away from what is acceptable, and that is even more evident when we raise the norm barrier. After all, it is simply not good enough that in the eyes of the world we maintain a semblance of virtue; it is even more necessary that also in our thoughts and desires the moral code must rule. But it is especially there that the pulsing power of evil is so irresistibly strong.

When we realistically look at where we are going, we are forced to confess that our life is on the verge of bankruptcy. That is evident in three ways. We do nothing to avert this deplorable state, and what is worse, we can't do anything about it. There simply is no hope that in the course of our years we will learn this because experience tells us that the progress we make is at best minimal. Nor is there ground to expect that our children will do a better job. On the contrary there is a fear that the next generation will face an even more difficult battle and suffer even greater defeat. And, in the third place, we simply cannot expect that after death, in the next life, we can try again to walk the long way that separates us from that ideal state. Our life drifts farther away from where we should go, instead of coming closer. Sadly we must admit that our life, in the sense of spiritual growth, must also be seen as a failure. For all appearances it may look splendid, it may seem a great success, but any deeper analysis must lead to the acknowledgment that we have not found its essential value. That's the reason why, throughout the history of the world, we hear without letup the compelling cry for deliverance, for setting us free.

CHAPTER FOURTEEN

The Redeemer

Throughout the history of the world, we hear without letup the compelling cry for deliverance, for setting us free. That's how the previous chapter ended. This statement now needs a closer examination.

In most religions known to us, the cardinal aim is human redemption. This deliverance is often expressed in very primitive ways. The general opinion is that evil spirits, demons, in all sorts of shapes and forms, dominate, and that these spirits in cunning ways can be deceived or, if that does not work, bribed and so be driven out. In many tribes and races we find elaborate ways of spirit worship, something that, as it were, permeates all of their life and influences every important act and resolution. Even though these simple religious reflections do point to the need for deliverance, they also show that the depth of the need is by no means fully gauged, that these actions do not at all promise any hope of true deliverance, something all humans in the ultimate depth of their souls long for.

The three major world religions are Buddhism, Islam, and Christianity. Of these three Buddhism is the oldest. This Indian religion started with the royal prince Siddhartha, born around the year 550 BC. When we investigate the prime ideas behind Buddhism, then it is at once clear that Buddha was very deeply touched by the suffering he saw everywhere in the world. No doubt his own experiences were a factor in this discovery. Born in a royal household, surrounded by luxury and beauty, he was only later in life exposed to life's underside, to sickness, death, and misery. It is understandable that this made a lasting impression on this young man. From that moment on he saw the gaiety of the court, the fun of feasts and partying, as a downright lie, as a denial of what, after all, constituted the only reality: suffering. It dawned on him that it would be better to leave the make-believe world of laughter and cheering and withdraw into the sacred places of truth and there unflinchingly embrace the suffering that dominated the life of every human from cradle to grave. What then is the cause of all that suffering? Buddha thought that the real source of suffering is desire – the desire for constancy, for durability, and for pleasure. The soul holds on to the tiniest bit of hope, looking for love, sensual satisfaction, passion. In short, the soul always clings to matters beyond her, goes on her knees trying to embrace a pseudo world and consequently falls into the trap of constant suffering. Is the world the cause of all that pain? No, the root lies much deeper: it lies in the soul itself, in that irrational longing, in that senseless passion. For even if the world would grant us all our desires, we still would not be happy, because we still would always want more. The desire for life, the urge for enjoyment, is like an inextinguishable fire: every wish granted leads to new desires.

How then can we escape that suffering? Only when that burning inner desire is silenced, when the soul returns to its starting point, and abandons the world, no longer desires, no longer yearns, no longer seeks, no longer chases, only then can we obtain peace and achieve rest. The soul, driven after death by her desire to enter into another body, descends in this way numberless times to earth, is then released from that obligation, is freed from that vicious cycle and quietly fades away in the Nirvana, where all existence is extinguished.

Buddha himself is, following this argument, the finder of truth. He is because he himself has traversed the long road of life to life and so has come to the final end. He was fully prepared for Nirvana, but, in order to redeem others, he, for a short time, denied himself the pleasure of entering there and preached the good news of deliverance to the suffering masses. In a sense he was not worried about his own fate; as far as he was concerned, salvation could pass him by. What is important is the truth, the ideas behind the truth, and of this truth he alone is the messenger, the prophet. He reawakens this knowledge in people.

That Buddha's followers in general have given such great honor to the personality of the founder of the religion was not Buddha's intention at all. By them the person was seen as greater than the message, the originator more important than his thinking. The reason for honoring the person rather than the message can mainly be traced to the fact that human suffering is far too great for an idea to be sufficient. His followers felt intuitively that Buddha's message alone was not nearly adequate to liberate them and extract them from the morass of suffering and sin. Buddha quite understandably underestimated this need. But history has clearly shown that humans are not satisfied in believing certain ideas; they also desire a Redeemer, an eternal force that truly can and will deliver – and this is a real human need.

Islam is of a much more recent date, born a thousand years after Buddhism. This religion sprouted in a totally different climate, and among different people. There where the merciless sun burns, in the endless deserts of Arabia, new religious ideas were developed that became the nucleus of this world religion. Islam adopted several elements from other religions, ranging from Judaism to Paganism, from Christianity to Eastern philosophy. Where Buddhism essentially bypasses God and can really function without a deity, for Islam the existence of the one and only god forms the cornerstone of its entire belief system. Allah alone is the all-powerful Authority. Who can challenge Allah? Who can question why Allah has created the world the way it is? We cannot, but must fear and worship him as the One and Only God. And what about redemption? Mohammed does not feel that the power of suffering is as important as Buddha, the Indian prince. When we surrender ourselves wholeheartedly to Allah, then our road to eternal bliss is assured. This surrender involves the keeping of the five all-important religious duties: confession of faith, prayer, the giving of alms, fasting, and the pilgrim trek to Mecca. Mohammed himself is no more than the bringer of the message, the prophet who has proclaimed the truth.

He is not the only prophet, not the first one, but he is the last and the most important one, the prophet par excellence.

It is typical that both religions approach deliverance by means of knowledge. Only the truth, the system of thought, sets free. Because once humans possess the truth and make it their own, they can fit it into their lives, suit it their way and even choose another path, a better one. The bankruptcy of our lives is especially focused in our total inability to acquire perfect knowledge and insight into our ultimate destination. There's more: the prophet alone preaches the truth and offers the possibility of salvation. We must apply this truth in our daily lives. By following the outlines given to us, we must deliver ourselves and find our way toward salvation. In other words, we could say that God redeems us, provided God sends the prophet who proclaims the truth. We are even more justified in saying that we can redeem ourselves if we only apply that truth, follow the way to truth; then we are on the way to salvation.

What then is so peculiar about Christianity? Christianity experiences the misery, the bankruptcy of life at a far deeper level, which is why it sees redemption differently from any other religion. Is it sufficient for us when we know the truth, when the road to salvation has been prescribed for us? No, because it doesn't work that way. I may be able to know exactly where to go but inside me there is a force that always pushes me to do evil. The good I know I do not do. The evil we do is not a mere matter of understanding, not an instance of ignorance, or some sort of deviance. There is much more that needs to change in us, because, as we have seen, the bankruptcy of our lives comes in three forms. We lack the knowledge, the insight into the truth. We also lack the peace, the true justice, the harmonious attitude to God. Finally we also lack the holiness, the will to do good. To be truly free we must surrender the entire structure of our existence: our redemption must be threefold, just as our misery is threefold.

CHAPTER FIFTEEN

Jesus, the Redeemer

When we set out to speak or write about Jesus, we are overwhelmed by painful experiences of inadequacy. It feels as if it is completely impossible to mention anything at all about him. When we do try to formulate some remarks about him, we can only succeed when our heart is totally at rest and our thoughts are intimately close to the reality of life's grand happenings. We can only try this in a moment of deep self-reflection, when life's illusions are seen in their proper perspective, and we stand in awe of the eternal truth.

First of all, we can say that we know about his personality from the Bible, in particular from the Gospels. In plain yet dignified language they picture his essence and his work for the sole purpose of making us all believe in him.

When we try to imagine him, it seems that our first impression is that of a humble person as he walks the roads of Galilee. What is it about him that moves us so unspeakably deeply? He stands outside the great life-bewitching scenario that keeps all others under its spell. He lives in a world of money, but money has no claim on his soul. He receives honor and praise, but also shame and rejection; but in him there is no trace of seeking human approval or being bitter because of the injustices others commit against him. He is just different; he is the true prophet who moves on a different plane altogether. Is that how you see him?

Maybe you have a different impression. If you look at him, if you read about him, then immediately you realize that now for the first time you notice what life is all about. He lives life to the fullest. That is evident in everything. He carries within him that golden nugget of knowledge because he sees God in everything. When he surveys the ever-changing panoramas, he at once visualizes the Father who adorned the grass of the fields with lilies. For him the entire world portrays God's majesty. Picture him in moments of deep sadness and of great gladness at Lazarus's grave; see him also when his disciples triumphantly return from their mission trip. In both cases he simply stands before the face of God, which does not involve a sudden transformation. He knows the Father in everything, in all of life's circumstances. We sense in his life the perfect peace, the true righteousness. Yes, at times there is tension between him and God. Still, as a child he lies down to rest as in the arms of God. Again picture him when, on one of those quiet summer nights, he unobtrusively abandons the rowdy masses to climb a mountain all by himself, to be alone with his Father. Yes, over whatever he does there is a glow of holiness. In all that he does he is totally different. In him life itself is reflected, life as it could be, life as it should be.

When we dig deeper into his life, then something strikes us that till now has not yet been quite clear. The first thing we notice is that he is truly human: the only human in whom true humanity is the most outspoken trait. When we get to know him more intimately, then we notice another major difference. Then we start to see him as so much at one with God, so much united with him, that the two increasingly become one. That is most striking when he speaks. His words come, as it were, directly from the heart of God. When he speaks we taste that unshakable absoluteness that can only originate from God. Jesus repels people and yet attracts them, and in both cases we sense that we are in the presence of the Most High Majesty of God himself.

In all this it is obvious that he himself is fully aware of this. He knows that his words are God's words, that he does the works of his Father. He affirms this himself when, with complete certainty, he says that whoever has seen him has seen the Father. Those who dwell with him day in and day out immediately feel the truth that, as Peter proclaimed: "You are the Son of the Living God because you have the words of eternal life." We can see God in a thousand things, in the cascading waterfall, in the thundering stream, in the enormous emptiness of the desert, in the magnificent manifestation of the clear starry night. God is everywhere. When you stand in front of Jesus, you look God straight in the eye: then we see him and he sees us. That is the secret of his personality.

To clarify this we could trace Jesus' entire life, but will instead concentrate on two matters that especially stand out: his authority and his love. There's no one like Jesus who can penetrate the innermost secrets of a person's life. His eyes have that stern and immense power, which is why some people secretly shy away from him. On the other hand many people are intensely attracted to him, like that Samaritan woman who had a long history of sinful living, or that rich young man who was not able or willing to do Jesus' bidding. Jesus also lashed out at people, and in righteous anger chastised them or, in a moment reduced a person's high self-opinion to proper proportions. He was forceful as no other has ever been forceful. But this difficult-to-gauge severity never had a trace of bitterness. When this woman at the well in Samaria heard Jesus telling her about the many men in her life, she was no doubt reminded of others who had accused her for the same reasons. She had been ostracized, despised as a woman whose company was not wanted, as one whose morals were despicable. She was familiar with all this and it had not bothered her. She knew very well that these same persons who anxiously avoided her as if she were unclean were not at all different from her. She wished she could turn the souls of these hypocrites inside out. All that sham behavior only caused bitterness in her. And there she stands facing Jesus. He pulls no punches; he exposes her life for the uselessness it was. And how does she react? She is shaken to the core. Why does facing this particular man make her so uneasy? It is because with Jesus there is something totally different. His severity represents the flames of God's holiness; his strictness burns deeply into her soul. With him we can experience that curious realization that we don't mind being chastised by him, being diminished under the crushing force of his judgments.

In addition to his strictness, there is also his generosity, his total compassion, which never is half-hearted, never weak, never sentimental, but always great, always majestic. Jesus is capable of reducing a person to nothing, till her soul is shattered, but he also can grab this same person, while crying for help, and embrace her with his unimaginable love. In one, long, terrifying speech he can lambast and precisely pinpoint the mean sins of the self-righteous Jews, and in the end lament: "Jerusalem, Jerusalem, how often I have longed to gather your children together as a hen gathers her chicks!" We can spend much time thinking about God, make all sorts of images and ideas regarding him, but when we find ourselves in the tightest spot ever, or when we start to discover what life really is all about, then it suddenly dawns on us: now I know how I must visualize God because he comes to us as Jesus. In the moments when life presents itself in its truest form, we need only look to the true God, the one we can see with our own eyes, the one whom we know when we look straight at Jesus.

None of the apostles felt this more strongly than John. That's why he gave Jesus that precious name: the Word. The Word expresses the essence of the soul. Jesus expresses the essence of God. He is the living visible Word. He is the eternal and only Son of God.

Each day the dispute and controversy around the person of Jesus is growing. And that makes good sense. If life were no more than a platform for some pleasant conversations and Jesus a person who had some new theories about God, then, sure, we could accept his words and his actions as mere information. But that is simply not the case; and Jesus, who stands with two feet on the earth, doesn't want that either. Jesus touches upon life in every facet. In every happening he draws the line to God. Therefore he is involved in every conflict that occurs in life. And in all this Jesus stands as God himself, smack in the middle of all others.

Jesus is especially concerned about us, the ordinary folk, those who live under the evil influence of the three idols. It's all about us, the people who shove and push, whose priority is to come out on top, and therefore vilify, injure, trample down, and so on. That's the sort of life in which Jesus engages himself. When he stands there in the midst of us, when he does that as the spark that is God, then this causes opposition everywhere. Jesus is always at the center of the conflict, even when it explodes around him with hurricane force.

If God were only some cozy, fragile idea dreamed up on a quiet summer night, we then could build him a beautiful golden shrine and once or twice during our lifetime make a pilgrimage there. But if God is like Jesus who like a fire touches all of life in all its movements and deliberations, if God stands right there in front of us and chastises us in his royal anger, if God is like that, then it is no wonder that we can only say time and again: I don't buy that kind of God! Then our right to life is at stake; then we have to fight over the last square foot. To deal with such a God is simply impossible. There's no place in our life for such a God; we have no use for him; he is our enemy. That's the reason why the conflict around Jesus grows, the turmoil intensifies, and everything involving him starts to arouse ever-greater discord. After all, life is not only words: deeds are even more important. Deeds are the wakeup call. Deeds are terrible and destructive. Deeds express the heart's desire.

Slowly but surely the opposition to Jesus grows. The atmosphere concerning him is filling with hate. Inevitably it leads to a terrible happening. The vicious result of our rejection is the cross. Here we are faced with the most violent deed we, the people of the world, have ever committed.

The very moment of Jesus' crucifixion contains one particular danger we tend to overlook. The real peril here is that Jesus, confronted with such a storm of hatred, would pronounce a bitter curse on humanity, would cut us loose, would reject us as unworthy of his love. There he hangs, suspended between God and us. There he is the butt of our hatred against God. Will he now cut all ties with humanity and retreat to God? Will he now abandon us, pronounce the curse on us and leave us to our devices, to certain death? We shudder when we ponder that possibility. Then Jesus' life would have been a horrible demonstration that we reject God, the living God as personified in Jesus. That would have been proof that God also would go without us, us hateful people, us dwelling in sin. That would mean that in him the tie that binds God and the world would be severed, that this connection would no longer be possible.

On the contrary, however, we now see in Jesus the miracle of all miracles: he refuses to condemn us. Our hatred is melted away in his love. Because of our sin he allows himself to be crucified, but in that act he keeps embracing us with his love. He carries the load of our sin and accepts this as a sacrifice out of misunderstood and unfathomable love. In all this he acts as God, acts out of God's love, who so loved the world, the cosmos. When we erred in our immense intoxication, God gave us him as the Word. When we recognized him as such, and when we rejected and crucified him, God responded to our action with his action: the great sacrifice. He took upon himself all our transgressions. In this way Jesus descended through the valley of all hellish death. He did it with an anxious heart. Has there ever been a human being that suffered as much as this holy, unique Son of Man? Never. In all his pain and suffering he looked past the screaming, hating human mass unto the Father who had requested this sacrifice from him. "The cup which the Father has given me, should I not drink it?" The Savior of the world bows down under the cross the Father has laid upon him.

That is a part of the Good News that has made an indelible impression on our consciousness of sin. He was crucified because of me. There are a lot of difficult-to-understand issues here, with one item standing out. What was the greatest sign of our rejection of God, what clearly was a sign of our curse, Jesus accepted from God's hand as a sacrifice and out of pure love made that curse his own. He offered himself unto death for the sake of our sins. Jesus is the world-priest who does not spare himself, who accomplishes the greatest-ever deed of sin-forgiving love: self-sacrifice. He stands between God and us and through the cross creates a new tie. He places our sinful hands in the hands of God the Father. In Jesus, God reconciled the world with himself. He is our peace.

With this as background the Gospels paint us the great and everlasting work of Jesus Christ. At one time the true followers of the truth possessed three distinct traits: knowledge, peace with God, and holiness. The tremendous loss we suffered through sin also came in three forms: our knowledge was affected by errors and ignorance, our peace with God turned into hostility and bitterness, and our holy character degenerated into filthy desire and self-indulgence. Over against these three rises up the human being Jesus, in whom God dwells, who himself is God, and in whom we see God himself.

He is the Word, the fiery arrow who has made it possible to know both God and ourselves. Jesus represents everything: he is the all and in all. He possesses all knowledge but he also gives the knowledge. He tells us about God: his entire being and the way he expresses himself clearly shows God's uniqueness. He is the only one who gives the insight: he is the Prophet.

However, this knowledge does not merely consist of words: this knowledge also collides with our heart, and bounces off against our unwillingness; this knowledge reveals our factual refusal to accept the cross. Our sinful self uses that cross as an opportunity to reject God. That's how we are by nature. Jesus, on the other hand, fulfills God's nature through his infinite sacrifice, accepting the cross as an offering laid upon him by the Father, for the payment of our sins. That cross, in the eyes of Jesus, is the carrying of the full load of our sin and God's wrath against our sin, so that he would make us right with God. It is he who offers peace: he is the Priest.

When he did this, when he reconciled our sinful and guilty human heart with God, he also entered the human soul as a silent guest to change it, to forever eradicate the immortal desire for sin, and to fill us with new life. He is the invisible King who, in the hearts of those who know and accept him, draws the contours of the new Life and the new Light. It is he who offers holiness: he is the King.

These three great benefits we owe to his work, which is also threefold. These three are represented in what Jesus calls the kingdom of God, which enters into human life as a strange phenomenon. It arrives in us when we see Jesus as a human being and recognize God in him. The Kingdom comes when we become aware of our terrible sin against that God (and his creation), of which the cross is the symbol, and when we, as his children, accept the unbelievable sacrifice of God's love fulfilled in Jesus. Then we bow down deeply, aware that we are nothing anymore, and when we see God in Jesus, God becomes everything in us. Jesus, who is the Word and God's executive in this world, speaks to us and works with us, and wants to make us new people.

In comparison with other religions, Christianity is far more conscious of human frailty. A prophet by himself cannot possibly save the human race, because in that case it's up to us to follow the indicated way. But the sorry part is that all of us are robbed of all that is true; we are wanderers, are totally to blame and, like slaves, chained to sin. Only another power can set us free, something impossible for us, impossible for any other human being. Only he can do it, the One who comes in the power of God. Time cannot elevate itself to eternity, nor can the finite become the Infinite, or the sinful become the Holy God. But what is possible is this: for God it is possible to embrace us again in spite of our sin; eternity can embrace time again, and the Creator can again pull the deeply lost creature to himself.

Christ is the hand of God who grabs the fallen humans and pulls them up. Christ is the mouth of God who whispers the great secrets in an unknowing heart. Christ is the power of God who breaks human powerlessness and makes humans pilgrims to the Light and heirs of the kingdom of heaven.

CHAPTER SIXTEEN

The Offered Salvation

When Jesus instructed his followers, his favorite subject was the kingdom of heaven. That particular heavenly kingdom is composed of all that life contains, the world and all that is. In the first place it has a connection to reason because it has to do with knowledge, the true knowledge that recognizes how God permeates all of life's experiences. In the second place it enters into the moral plane because it expresses in continually stronger terms that we must serve God in a child-like way. Finally it also encompasses the large spiritual, religious field: peace with God, the compassionate Father who forgives our sins. Because the kingdom of heaven consists of these three components, it causes persons to become totally different; it brings them back to their original destination.

In certain ways we can state that every person has a basic longing for what the kingdom of God has to offer. The reason is that the benefits the Kingdom offers were, at one time, part and parcel of the human condition and therefore part of our genetic makeup and still dormant there. The vacuum left there points to our royal birth. On the other hand, however, we are in the process of abandoning the Kingdom features, are continually sliding back, are always backing away from the true, eternal good. It is true that in our hearts we always retain a certain dissatisfaction, which at times can seriously affect us, but the problem is that we tend to look for a solution in completely wrong directions. We seek remedy in knowledge and are all too soon satisfied when we acquire external, superficial insight. We also try to infuse a bit of holiness into the matter but there too we far too soon stop looking, convinced that in comparison with others we have made enough progress. As for making peace with God, there too we are quickly convinced that this will easily fall into place as well. We sometimes sense the lack of peace, and in the depth of our hearts this emptiness hurts, but in the hurly-burly of daily life we soon manage to soothe our feelings. That's why we usually avoid matters concerning the kingdom of heaven and turn to the much more enticing idols.

It should be noted that several circumstances conspire to continually obscure the absence of the Kingdom in our lives. We humans are always inclined to blame the cause of our suffering and misery on powers beyond our influence. We partly blame it on the people we associate with. If only they were different; if only they would show more love and sincerity, then our lives too would be much better and purer. In our greatly depraved society, we reason, nobody can actually live a perfect life and everybody eventually becomes a callous self-seeker, because the basis for happiness simply has vanished. In our holy zeal we try to bring about the most radical changes in society in the hope that these measures will cause a happy ending. We are puzzled when, in spite of all these changes, our society remains sinful and life fails to improve. What we overlook is that the great sin, the cause of all our misery, cannot be traced to others, and even less to "society," but solely to ourselves, to our defects, to our guilt. As much as possible, we want to blame our shortcomings on others and on institutions outside us. We continually want to rid ourselves of all blame, while the only route to real salvation is that we fully own up to our guilt, admit that the emptiness dwells in our own soul. To put it differently: we are inclined to explain our suffering in such a way that we are victims of hostile powers outside ourselves. Our victim-obsession deprives us of the real incentive to essential conversion. Thus the first thing we have to do is to recognize that we are totally on the wrong track, that our lives completely lack a goal, that we ourselves are entirely to blame, and that the fundamental fault lies first of all within ourselves. Only then have we arrived at the heart of the matter.

The heart of the matter consists again of three conditions. We have an innate desire to learn. Our daily prayer should be: "Free me from my ignorance, my stupidity, and my erroneous ways." St. Augustine's famous dictum was: "I long to know God and my soul." We roam in the fog of unknowing, we fail to see our future, we have no idea where we are going and where we come from, we have no inkling that our beginning and our end is in God. In every respect we are imprisoned, clueless, at a loss. We are unable to acquire that knowledge; it's impossible for us to force open the gates that provide insight into the truth, because in these matters we are powerless. This comes only when we find Christ, the prophet, the Word of God; this comes only when we listen and surrender to him. When we hear and read and experience his words, then, deep in our soul, we feel that this is the truth. The great act that brings salvation is surrender – the desire to receive, the urge to listen.

The same applies to the second and equally important question. Many of us thirst for justice, for the harmonious relationship with God, for shalom.

How do we free ourselves from guilt when it seems that we are banned from God's presence and burdened under the load of our sin? How do we approach him? How do we, in full confidence, look up to him who is our gracious Father? There too it is simply not possible for us to rely on our own devices. There too we cannot pull ourselves up by our bootstraps. We are unable to come up with the right excuses; we cannot show God that we have certain virtues that will pave the way to salvation; in no way can we stifle the voice of our guilt by ourselves. We by ourselves cannot open the gate that leads to the peace that passes understanding. Only when our soul finds Christ is it possible for hope to emerge. He is the Redeemer, he is our peace. In him we find the answer to that thirst for righteousness. Only when we learn to meet him in that way will we know him and sense that he is the One. The one great act that will bring salvation is the surrender, the will to receive and the desire to listen.

And when we pose the third question, "How do we get rid of our evil heart?" then there too the result is the same. It is simply foolishness to assume that we are able to radically change so that we can walk as perfect saints. That sort of sainthood is just not up for grabs, and it is remarkable that, the more we try to pursue it, the more we discover that we are chasing the impossible. True, we usually are on our guard for big and ostentatious sins, but it always boils down to that heart of ours. It is precisely there where all these dirty, impure, and untruthful thoughts originate. We have to find the beautiful Christ, the king of our souls. Our hearts have to loudly cry out: rule us, direct us! O God, equip us with your power. We simply cannot walk alone on the long and difficult road to holiness; we are incapable of completely changing ourselves: we must become changed, we must allow ourselves to be changed. Only when our lives are touched by Christ is it possible for us to feel new power stir in us, a new force that says: "The old me does not live anymore: now Christ lives in me." The ultimate act that brings on salvation is surrender, the will to receive, the listening to his voice.

To put it differently: the ultimate saving act does not consist of successful accomplishments and immense zeal, but first and foremost involves the humble deed of surrender. That is the secret of all salvation. Once this surrender has in fact taken place, then God is again central to our lives. God is the one who will give us knowledge, righteousness, and holiness. These saintly forces stream down from above while we are lifted up to eternity. Christ is the hand that helps us to meet God, and he hands all this to us. It is only by surrender that we come into possession of these eternal benefits.

Finally, this surrender is what usually is called faith. Faith is not just a matter of rational acceptance but especially a matter of trust, and again, of surrender. Of course it includes our intellect, but the use of our brainpower serves as the catalyst to accomplish surrender.

The decisive factor in all this is the acceptance of Jesus' hand.

Drowning in ignorance, rejected by God, and wallowing in unholiness, our soul clings to the final and sole solution: our surrender to God's grace. He either will accept me or reject me. O God, help me; grab me and rescue me. Forgive me and give me strength!

Jesus Christ, eternal light, be to me a prophet, a priest, and a king.

CHAPTER SEVENTEEN

Why We Are Here

When we observe the life of the average person, we soon notice that it can only be thought meaningful when it is seamlessly part of the greater context, when it is a segment of a larger entity in which it fits perfectly. Then it makes sense, then it has meaning, then it plays a useful role.

The life of each of us is, indeed, a subsection, a tiny trickle in that broad, immense, and mighty river of the life of humanity in its entirety. That human life has existed for many millennia, and has subdivided itself into nations and different races, and even now is still subject to the most drastic changes. The great and difficult question all thinkers wrestle continually with is this: Has human life a purpose, does it really make sense, is there a permanent meaning? Does life have a destination? Will something come out of it? Have all these centuries, all these happenings, all these wars and discoveries, have they been useless, or may we assume that the history of the world is the realization of a plan that will result in something concrete? And if that is the case, if we may see the history of the world as having a meaningful purpose, as something that has a definite goal, what then is the destination? Where do we end up? Does all this make sense?

We can divide the answers to these questions into three categories.

The most optimistic of these is that the history of the world is one of continual progress. Slowly but surely we, as humanity, find ourselves on the road to constant improvement. We evolved from being uncouth savages to cultured beings wherein life takes on an ever-higher and a more refined form. The Egyptian and Babylonian era was followed by the Greek and Roman period, and our new world was based on the finest of the Greek civilization. Progress is a continuous process, ever higher, ever more beautiful in expression. When we question this theory and wonder wherein we, as humans, are progressing, then the answers are different. Some claim that we enjoy more freedom. Those early times were dominated by despotism: the ruler owned it all, but slowly the glory time of freedom emerged. Others will assert with equal force that knowledge advanced, and people became more charitable and more united. In antiquity it was nation against nation, person versus person. True, now too the world is divided, but then we are not yet at the end of the road. There still is progress. There is the increase in knowledge: simply amazing. We also are a lot richer and know much more in the technical field. If our ancestors could see what we are able to do, they would think that we had become angels or gods. Everywhere there is development and progress. Where will it end? It apparently will end when humanity has reached its highest levels, the ultimate in knowledge, in technical know-how and human desire. At that stage we will be one, the dawn of the true culture. When will that come? Nobody knows. But it looks more and more likely that our culture, based as it is on self-satisfaction, will at a certain moment collapse and then we as humanity will face a worldwide calamity that will occur without warning. It may yet take a while, but there's no doubt that it will come. We then can look forward to that "new birth."

Totally opposite to this is the position of those who occupy the pessimistic point of view. According to this point of view when it comes down to it, nothing is good anymore. Of course, communication now has never been easier, but this really amounts to very little. We would prefer to do away with all this rigmarole for a bit of true human happiness. Where it concerns the most important human interests, we lose ground continually. And that makes sense. Our lifestyle increasingly distances us from our natural life where we lived by our instincts. Our current way of living can be carried on for a long time, but eventually this takes its toll through growing unrest and dissatisfaction. We no longer are happy, no longer at ease, and we are losing our naturalness.

Do we really think that we have gained in virtue? When we observe society, what we really see is more self-interest, more immorality, more greed, and greater sensuality. Don't we see that all these forces have gained momentum year after year, century after century? Today the wars are much more intrusive and comprehensive than earlier ones. It is undeniably a fact that the world regresses more and faster than ever before. Global degeneration increases by leaps and bounds. The history of the world is one of regression, of deterioration and growing depravity. The end of it all is that the entire creation, worn out by human abuse, reverts back to the eternal rest of the state of nothing, into the immobility of death.

Apart from these two one-sided points of view, there is a third option that deals with the heart of the matter. Whether there is progress or not avoids the real issue. Within a certain timeframe we can indeed talk about progress and development, but history teaches us that every cultural system after a certain time goes under and disintegrates. Time and again we see new forms of civilization and new ideas that for a short time find enthusiastic reception, but all of them contract and slink away to make place for new possibilities. That's the main reason why, in general, we cannot speak of progress. The history of the world is one of continuous birth, of growth and death, of rise and fall. There is no continuous upward line. There is no lasting gain, no real positive outcome. For a while we gain some spiritual benefits and then they too fade away again. Every religion, every philosophy, every social and political system, every thought pattern enjoys a period of growth and then slowly disappears and dies. To question a purpose and to ask for some sense is completely foolish and unreasonable. The meaning of life is life itself. According to Spengler, "all looking for a deeper meaning is fruitless."

When we compare these three different ways of looking at life, it becomes plain that the question we are dealing with is not an easy one. What really goes on in world history? Where does it all lead to and where does it end?

The matter is too large to precisely outline, so I will confine myself to some brief remarks.

First of all, in the last few centuries we have seen an ever-greater convergence. It looks as if there is a beginning of greater uniformity. In earlier times the various cultural entities were totally separate. Nobody in Rome had a clue what China was all about, and those in the Americas knew nothing about India. Human life went on in different streams, beside each other yet totally apart. There was no connection, no unity. As such we really could not speak of a united humanity.

If the miracles of our technological society have altered one important matter, then it certainly is the matter of a unified humanity. Need I mention the telegraph, the telephone, or the radio, all instruments that make it possible to communicate with distant locales more quickly than ever before in history? Within minutes we are notified of what happens in Paris or Washington. The life of the nations has become local. There are no more walls that protect any culture against foreign influences. Nobody today speaks anymore of the unbridgeable gap between East and West now that the East is West and the West is East. The world is one, one humanity, one body, one totality. That is a miracle of which we by any stretch of our imagination cannot possibly fathom its ultimate consequences. We only now begin to understand the boundless changes that this phenomenon has for the many millions in Asia and Africa who for centuries have lived in isolation. What is in store for the world? One world empire? One world culture? Will we see a leveling of the deep-seated differences? Can we expect a meeting of minds between these so divergent views? Will East and West really become one? Whatever it may be or become, we are witnessing one of the world's most miraculous moments: humanity itself is engaged in intertwining itself into one body.

In the second place, every thought that history is a process leading to more freedom, greater happiness, love, and perfection is pure fantasy. There is nothing in history that suggests this. Time and circumstances change, but the core of the matter does not. We humans don't become better, happier, or more satisfied. It would be nice if this were the case, but that's not how it is. Cultural progress has little or nothing to do with moral advancement. What really seems to be the case is that every step forward we take in one direction is negated by regress in other matters.

If we want to draw a line through the unpredictable events happening in the world, then it is my belief that we can only do this in the way the gospel deals with this. The Good News shows us that the history of the world, from its very inception, is dominated by two factors. To recognize these criteria even after many millennia will give us some insight into the meaning of the world, and why we are here.

The first factor is that of sin, of human self-deification. This phenomenon in the development of human cultures repeatedly takes on new forms. It reveals itself in the ascetic Eastern religions as a desperate attempt to become so unified with the deity that believers will experience the power of the Creator in their own bodies. That same sort of self-deification also was the dream of the builders of the Tower of Babel and today it is apparent in the fervent desire for having a worldwide reach. It also undergirded the culture of antiquity, which aimed for a culture of harmonious rationality. Today it is the driving force behind our Western world. In the course of the centuries the theme of human divinity displays itself in very different forms and is now more and more becoming a reality. In essence it is the burning desire for power, and we know that we now possess so much power that it goes far beyond the wildest dreams. We also have an immense drive to know more, and that urge has resulted in greater and deeper insight far beyond what we could have imagined earlier. At the basis of all this is the attempt to make the powers of nature subservient to us so that we humans can succeed in our aim of world domination. Indeed, we rise higher and higher on the road of attaining human divinity.

Already we see the contours of the end times. The end manifests itself in an increasing and senseless chaos among the human race in ways far greater than ever before experienced. In the very end, thoroughly evil elements will use the powerful instruments of modern technology to make life totally machine-dominated. Johan Huizinga's book *In the Shadow of Tomorrow* depicts that sort of scenario, outlining the anxiety-provoking impasse in which we find ourselves. Fairy tales about "world peace" and the approaching "state of bliss" now look more foolish than ever. The younger generation grows up in the certainty that we face a hard and grim future. In one of Vondel's dramas we find these lines:

Heilig, heilig, nog eens heilig	Holy, Holy, once more Holy.
Driemaal heilig, eer zij God	Triple Holy, to God be praise.
Buiten Hem is 't nergens veilig	Outside him there is no refuge.
Heilig is het groot gebod	Holy is the great command.

If I were to characterize something that as an awful certainty becomes more evident every day based on the current world situation, then I would express it in the terms Vondel used: "Outside him there is no refuge."

The self-deification of us humans, in whatever form, whether it is in the expression of a mystic rendering of Divine unity, or in the ideals of world rule, or by means of cultural advancement and scientific achievements – all this, always and inevitably, leads to deep and tragic failure. Essential salvation, therefore, is only possible when we go again to where we belong in the framework of creation, when we occupy the place allotted to us as children of God.

The second factor the Good News points to regarding the world's history is God's act of grace. Amidst the turmoil we cause, the Supreme God is busy weaving in the plan of his Kingdom, the kingdom of grace in Jesus Christ. It is through this Kingdom that we are taught to deeply bow down before the face of our king. It is a Kingdom that traverses the path of the world's history along a Via Dolorosa, a road of sorrows, just as the Lord of the kingdom, Jesus himself, traveled this road of sorrows. Today our human kingdom is becoming more appealing, as it increasingly conforms to the secular world, as it is being sucked deeper and deeper into the attractions of secularity. Yet in spite of this, God keeps on carrying and directing this world. In the last book of the Bible, Revelation, we find the dramatic description of the form the end crisis of the kingdom of this world will take. There too we can read in tender terms and with baited breath how, in words that defy description, the end of all things will come, when God is all and in all.

CHAPTER EIGHTEEN

The Completion of Life

The final question to be dealt with is the completion of our personal lives. Are we immortal? Is there life after death? Where are we going? What is behind that strange, mysterious curtain that we usually call death? This question too has a long and remarkable history.

In the first place it is fitting to mention that almost all the world's religions have believed in a life after death. However they pictured this, whether they supposed that souls would float as phantoms on earth or would seek refuge far away, whether souls returned to this earth in new and different life forms, or whether they were at once transformed to a state of greater or lesser sanctification, behind all this was always the steadfast conviction that after death our life would not completely disappear but would, as it were, continue in a different form of existence.

The question that arises is why this belief has been so generally accepted. This question can be answered in several ways with particular emphasis on the following.

In the first place many distinctly feel that this life has in all aspects the character of a fragment. It is not complete, not a finished entity. That is clear when we consider that not everything hidden in our souls is capable of being expressed. There are inclinations, desires, higher needs that are crowded out by the lower motives of self-preservation and the struggle for our daily bread and similar causes. It's often the case that the most desirable, that which makes us most truly human, remains deeply hidden and cannot come out in the open. That gives us a feeling of incompleteness, a notion that our lives lack a degree of dignity. This is not a matter of good or bad, it is worse than that: it makes life look small and insignificant. We sense that and say: there must be more to life than this. In not a single aspect does life reflect a ripe fruit, although it does have the unmistakable sign of a bud, a blossom. Even more pronounced, many people have the distinct feeling that life resembles a dream, sometimes a scary dream, or at times a pleasant one, but never more than a dream. At the same time they are convinced that what we call dying is nothing but an awakening, a transition from a dream situation to that of the real phase.

In addition, it is true that the human notion of what is just fails to find fulfillment in this life. Life is always different from what we expect and desire. The scale of justice is hardly ever in balance. That too has contributed to the thought that there's more to life than we experience. There simply must be more that still is for us terra incognita, unexplored terrain.

The Egyptians, in the time of the pyramids, used multiple symbolic illustrations. They quite realistically showed how the soul in the realm of the dead was judged and only then was given permission to appear before the king of the gods. That sort of thinking, involving a judgment after death or a bridge over which the dead must cross, is actually a worldwide phenomenon. It shows us that the human soul harbors a deep and ineradicable consciousness that everybody must submit to a righteous judgment.

Finally, every human carries in his or her soul an intuitive longing for eternity. In the midst of the currents of life's happenings we sense something of the eternal. Precisely because we experience the perishable, the passing of time, the change of seasons, this actually is proof that we possess something that exceeds the temporal, something eternal.

These three considerations seem to confirm the instinctive notion that there is something in us humans that suggests there is more to death than meets the eye. That notion is alive in many other ethnic groups and it is likely that the idea will persist.

Even though there is a common belief in life after death that has lasted throughout the ages, the opinions concerning what happens after death differ significantly. Without going into precise details, it is fitting to conclude with what the Gospels teach us concerning these matters.

The Good News shows us that there are two ways open for us: the possibility of going this way alone, apart from Christ, and walking this road with him. In the former, we are on our own and live based on the principles of our own nature. And since that nature, as has been shown earlier, is tied to ignorance, to error, guilt, and weakness, this condition of "being alone" can best be described as being tied to the "kingdom of darkness" (Colossians 1:13). That word "darkness" in the Bible has everywhere a frightening connotation, which we immediately grasp without even being able to exactly realize what this condition actually means. "To be in Christ," on the other hand, immediately conveys something grand and beautiful. This phrase describes persons who in the depth of their lostness have clung to Christ, the great Savior of their lives. As of that moment these people live, as it were, within his aura, are enclosed by his protecting presence, carried by the glow that emanates from him. For all human beings those are the only two possibilities.

What really happens at the moment of death is difficult to describe. Death can best be called the gate allowing entry to the realm of truth. In death all pseudo-values and pseudo-powers disappear and the soul falls back to its ultimate reality. Then and there, what was already present but still hidden in layers of uncertainty and twilight is revealed.

In death all doors to perishable life are closed for good. The eye cannot distinguish anything anymore about the shape and size of visible matters, the ear can no longer interpret the sounds that flow from this world. All doors to the material world fall shut; even thinking in the common sense ceases to function, connected as it is to the multitude of our bodily functions. In the same way this also applies to the soul, just as we experience this when evening falls. Stars shine all day long but during the daylight we cannot observe them because their light is obliterated by the stronger sunlight. However, as soon as in the evening the sun goes down we see the stars twinkle everywhere in the heavens. So it is with the soul. As soon as the portals of the soul to the material world are irrevocably closed and the soul itself is silenced because no more images rise up from the unconscious, then the Light of all lights, the spiritual world of God and his angels, starts to shine. The soul finds itself taken up into a different sphere, as matters that earlier seemed unrealistic now become the supreme reality. The material world disappears from under her feet, so to say, and ends up in other, newer life possibilities. Of course, God was present before in our lives. He now dwells in and around us all the time, but in the clamor of this world we could not detect his voice and in the glamour of this world we could not see his light. But now when all the other interventions have fallen away we confidently can rely on him as the only certainty.

When we have dwelled on earth in the state of self-reliance, when we with both hands have indulged in sensual matters and in their powerful attractions, then the moment of death is an instance of immense horror. In all our days we have shut God out of our daily life, have hated and rejected him and have withdrawn from his protective hand. Now the doors to the matters we can experience go closed and only God remains. We then experience God's light, and immediately our soul is gripped by an anxiety that goes beyond description. We want to flee but we cannot. There is no way out, nothing to hold on to. Then a colossal and all-encompassing terror grips us, something beyond words but which occasionally occurs when nightmares torture us. Then we experience an agony so strong and so intense that it saturates us with emotions of immeasurable suffering.

On the other hand, it is possible that in this life we have dwelled "in Christ." Although while dwelling on earth we often have been seduced by the attraction of carnal desires, we nevertheless in our heart of hearts have used a different approach, because the power of Christ has carried us and his nearness has made us steadfast, because in all our life we've had a genuine longing for him and a thirst for communion with him. Every sinew of our existence was permeated with a longing for God, as the greatest good. In that case death will be seen as the great revelation. Perhaps the soul may first experience some timidity, some hesitancy. But as soon as we detect the lights, as soon as we see the reflection of God's presence in the distance, then an infinite joy will be born in us. Is that You, O eternal magnificence who always has been the object of my searching? With inexpressible rapture I will flee to him and embrace him as my all, as my salvation. And observing him, the pure sight of him and his glory, I will go from joy to greater joy, from light to greater light. In the joyfulness I will then experience lies the hallmark of eternity, because God is eternal. At that same moment the miraculous power of God's Spirit will sanctify me so that every single spot of sin will be washed away.

That's how we could imagine the way we enter eternity. It is impossible, of course, to paint a precise picture here.

For those with eyes to see and ears to hear, they already can detect the first glimmers of eternity in their lives. It can suddenly overwhelm us, this longing, this intense yearning for what soon will be revealed.

Our salvation does not consist of eloquent words or of great accomplishments. Our salvation only depends on entering into God's nearness, in observing him who personifies salvation. Our soul never tires of him. He is the rest and the life, the power and the peace, the joyfulness and the delight.

As rudderless ships we all roam the somber sea of life, sometimes severely in motion, then again in quietness. Sometimes pounded to bits against the rocky shore or sucked away into swirling whirlpools. Life always looms large and is often frightening. But those in the know set the correct course; they hold on to Jesus as the only guide to salvation. Only in him is the knowledge and the peace and the holiness. Those who believe in him have eternal life.

If you know all these things in your heart, you are saved when you do them . . .

www.ingramcontent.com/pod-product-compliance
Lightning Source LLC
Chambersburg PA
CBHW031226170426
43191CB00030B/284